THE GREAT

CULTURE
[DIS]CONNECT

Building a Business Culture that Works

THE GREAT

CULTURE
[DIS]CONNECT

Building a Business Culture that Works

written by

MARY E. MARSHALL

Indigo River Publishing

Editors: Jackson Haynes and Regina Cornell
Book Design: mycustombookcover.com

Indigo River Publishing
3 West Garden Street, Ste. 352
Pensacola, FL 32502
www.indigoriverpublishing.com

Ordering Information:
Quantity sales: Special discounts are available on quantity purchases by corporations, associations, and others. For details, contact the publisher at the address above.

Orders by US trade bookstores and wholesalers: Please contact the publisher at the address above.

Printed in the United States of America

Library of Congress Control Number: 2018959988
ISBN: 978-1-948080-48-4

First Edition

With Indigo River Publishing, you can always expect great books, strong voices, and meaningful messages. Most importantly, you'll always find . . . words worth reading.

To all those inspirational, hardworking entrepreneurs who lead with values—this book is a celebration of you and your dedication to company culture.

Table of Contents

Preface: ix

Case Study: Automation Engineers 1

Chapter One: Why Does Culture Matter? 9

Chapter Two: Intentional Culture vs. Unintentional Culture 17

Chapter Three: How to Identify Your Values 27

Chapter Four: Owning the Values in Your Business 37

Chapter Five: Hiring for Values and Cultural Fit 47

Chapter Six: Role of the CEO as Culture Strategist 61

Chapter Seven: Culture Change 73

Chapter Eight: The Legacy of a Culture 85

There is a lot of talk about business culture but not a lot of con-sensus as to how to create a "thriving culture." *Thriving* is usually defined as being profitable, growing, returning money to owners and shareholders, and attracting and retaining talent, and a thriving business is generally described as a great place to work. There are literally millions of how-to books on each of these individual topics but relatively few that map out the process of defining the values of an organization and then creating a great intentional culture on top of that.

This is that book. For every small to mid-sized business that wants to grow and create a legacy beyond the founder, this book will outline the steps. More importantly, it explains why this is so import-ant to the success of the business and how without it chaos reigns.

CEOs often talk about their culture but ultimately don't under-stand what it is or how it was created. They don't understand what intentional versus unintentional culture is, and they don't know what to do when they hire a cultural misfit, let alone a cultural terrorist.

The Great Culture [Dis]Connect will lead you through the process of defining, instituting, and leading an intentional culture grounded in values for success. As with any business book that's worth reading, it's short and story-based so that entrepreneurs can quickly absorb and implement the ideas into their companies.

AUTOMATION ENGINEERS

Automation Engineers was started in 1989 by an entrepreneur who was fed up with inefficient workplaces. He was an engineer by training and had a knack for solving problems in workplace automation systems, which launched his career at IBM. Realizing he hated being told what and how to do things, he branched off on his own, taking a few engineers with him to start his company. His original mission was to solve those workplace automation issues that no one else could solve.

The founder did not start with a strategic plan or any particular vision in mind, other than to create great systems and products. His seed money was all his own, and he really enjoyed going to work every day, creating things and working with people he liked. The company grew from a few million in revenue to $29M by 2018. However, most of that growth happened early on, and since then, rather than hockey-stick growth, the company went up and down like a yo-yo and could not seem to grow more than two years in a row without a significant setback of some sort. This year would prove no different.

The CEO, Roger, was getting up there in years and was completely fed up that the majority of his peers from IBM had not only moved on and started other companies but had passed him up long ago in the revenue column. In fact, most had crossed over the $100M mark and been sold, moving on to start other businesses or sailing on a yacht in the Seychelles with more money and freedom than Roger could even dream of.

Roger was particularly frustrated that his company seemed to be a revolving door of talent, that some of their good clients were literally dying out, and that no matter what he did to change things the outcome was always the same. He wanted to be done with the company but couldn't really bring himself to do anything about it other than complain. Where he once could see a complex set of problems, now he only saw a pain-in-the-ass bunch of employees that he had to pay. Although Roger was technically quite competent—even considered brilliant—his ability to confront or deal with people issues was nonexistent.

He had about one hundred employees in a few different states and, for the most part, was pretty hands-off on the day-to-day running of the business—unless people didn't do things his way. He had a knack for telling people to think for themselves and innovate, but when they did he shot them down and made them feel like they were sitting for a PhD dissertation defense. Or, more likely, he would have the COO convey his displeasure.

The company was ran day to day by the COO, Julianna, who was rumored to have once had an affair with Roger, but no one knew for sure. Neither were married now, so it wouldn't have mattered, but it was always the subject of rampant speculation among the employees. Roger wanted to promote Julianna to CEO because he was tired of the responsibility, but she demurred and said she was happy with her role and could never be qualified for such a role. She had been with the company for twenty-five years, starting as the receptionist. She had no formal education and dropped out of high school to get married. She was universally despised and ridiculed by the staff, especially the engineers as she frequently referred to them as her "big brains," to which they said behind her back that they had to make up for her lack of one. Julianna was the only one who had not heard this joke, including the company's customers and vendors. To say she was naïve would not be accurate, because she had an uncanny ability to manipulate people, but she was truly and utterly incurious about the company's products, customers, and marketplace. If you got on her bad side, you would be targeted and gone within a month. Whenever it became known that Julianna was displeased with someone, an office pool would start with bets on when that person would be gone.

The current strategic plan, which called for sales of $40M and the sale to a strategic partner in two years, was stalled out. Julianna was doing what she always did when this happened: looking to cut expenses anywhere she could find them. Ironically, salaries were not one of those places. She paid people in the mid to high range for their positions, and if someone threatened to leave and Roger let her know that person was a "keeper" (as he referred to those whom he did not want to lose), she would constantly raise their pay. The result was that people who started out as she did, with no formal education or training, would end up making twice what they could elsewhere, and so they were reluctant to leave. Those who were qualified realized what a horrible place it was to work and left because they could get equally well-paying jobs elsewhere without the extreme dysfunction at Automation Engineers. Word in the industry was that although the company had some legacy products and systems that were definitely best in class when they came out, nothing they had produced in the last five years had reached the same level of success as their older products.

On top of all the other drama, Julianna had just hired a new person for the accounting department. The CFO was apoplectic, as this person's sole work experience was as the ticket taker at the movie theater where Julianna had just seen a movie. Julianna thought she showed spark, so she hired her as the AP/AR clerk. Normally, a background check would have been required for this position, but Julianna decided that she could forgo it this time, as this person represented a diversity hire and Julianna felt she was giving back to the community by hiring her. To the employee's credit, she continued to tell everyone she was not qualified but welcomed the opportunity to learn. The CFO bit his tongue and reluctantly agreed to train her. Julianna also thought she could help with HR, but the HR manager flat out refused to let this happen, which set up a silent war between the HR manager and Julianna. The HR manager became the latest person added to the office pool.

The sales, marketing, and engineering departments all had competent heads. To Roger they were keepers, and they had figured out how to stay out of Julianna's way to get their jobs done. They called it a "Julianna-rama" when she decided to redecorate, remodel, or re-org one of the departments. When this happened, some openly joked that she and Roger must be on the outs, so she was trying to prove herself to him. If they were involved, it was the worst-kept secret on the planet; if they weren't, they weren't doing anything to dissuade people. Whether they were or weren't intimately involved was really irrelevant to the day-to-day operations, but more broadly it affected everyone's perception of Roger's judgment (or lack thereof), Julianna's competence, and the company's ability to achieve the goals on its strategic plan. The managers were hoping the company could be bought out and that new, competent management would come with a sale.

Roger decided to engage an investment banking firm to assess the value and help find a strategic buyer. As with everything in this company, news spread quickly. It was one of the few times that Julianna was not in the loop on the decision, and her behavior quickly escalated from a Julianna-rama to a bat-shit-crazy cyclone that ultimately threatened to take everyone down with it. Roger was finally ready to move on strategically, but Julianna could not see beyond today.

The industry trade show day was approaching and a "new" product was being rolled out. Realistically, it was an old product with a new package—not innovative, but different enough that customers might see it that way. The engineers kept saying the product timeline was not right, not enough testing had happened, and they were not ready to demo it at the show. Julianna insisted that they were ready, and in fact, she would prove it by demonstrating it herself. The sales and engineering teams were horrified, as she had never actually displayed any interest, let alone knowledge, as to how any of their products worked. They appealed to Roger and strongly cautioned him that this could be an epic fail. Roger said he had faith in Julianna and if she wanted to deliver this at the show, they should support her and not let her fail. In fact, he was so confident in her that he invited a few of the strategic partners (potential buyers) whom the investment banker had identified to see his team in action.

Once Julianna knew that Roger had invited the potential buyers to her presentation at the show, she was determined that the team would be ready. She was conflicted, however, because she didn't want Roger to sell, as she saw no role for herself in the new company, but she did want to impress Roger and the rest of the disbelieving team and prove that she knew what she was doing. She was determined to prove all of them wrong.

Julianna had never presented before, so she insisted on using teleprompters with everything she needed to say. She also insisted that an engineer be on stage with her to operate the equipment. However, two days before the show the engineers informed her that they had found a significant bug in the product and it would not be fixed by the show. She said she didn't care, "fix it or you are ALL fired." They worked for forty-eight hours straight trying to figure things out but could not make it work, so they pulled the new features of the product out and re-did the presentation so that essentially they would be reintroducing an old product. Their calculation was that Julianna would not know the difference; she didn't read anything and knew nothing about their products. They thought it would actually be sort of funny to set her up. They knew Roger was looking to sell the company, and some were even trying to figure out how they could put together an offer to buy it.

Meanwhile, the CFO was noticing significant discrepancies in the accounting department. Cash flow had been tough in some years, but they always kept $2M in a reserve account to handle the fluctuation. He was having to dip into it almost every month, yet sales were consistent. One top of that, the bankers were doing an audit, as was the state department for sales tax. He was busy gathering the documents for both of those parties and not paying attention to the decreasing cash flow.

The day of the presentation, Julianna needed to be at her best. She was on display for all of those who had doubted her over the years. In twenty-five years she had never spoken to a customer or attended a single trade show, so she was not really prepared for the pressure or the pace.

She was inappropriately dressed, more ready for a cocktail party than a presentation, and insisted that she did not need to practice with the engineers as she knew what she was doing. When it came time for her to unveil the "new" product, she gamely began reading the teleprompter while the engineer operated the device and the software. The engineer figured out before Julianna did that the words she was saying were for the product that was not ready, not the product he was demonstrating. When the confused faces and murmurs from the audience started, Julianna was oblivious because she was just so thrilled by her ability to read from the teleprompter. The engineer tried to get her to stop by motioning to her that there was a problem. When she finally noticed that he was motioning to her, she dismissed him as her big-brained engineer and told him he had nothing to worry about. He walked off the stage. At this point the murmur had become more like a roar and people were laughing and shaking their heads in disgust on their way out. The 250 people in the audience were gone twenty minutes into a forty-five-minute presentation.

Julianna was furious with the engineers, but really didn't understand what had happened. What she did know was that people were laughing at her and that an engineer had walked off the stage. She found the engineer and fired him on the spot. As a result, three other engineers quit that day as well, as did the entire sales team that was at the show. Fortunately for them, there were plenty of other competitors at the show who were interested in talking with them about job opportunities.

Roger had not attended the show; he felt he didn't need to be present since his right-hand Julianna was there. Several old friends of Roger's (those who grew much more successful businesses) called him to find out what had happened. He was in the dark but was about to be illuminated.

When Roger called Julianna, she burst into tears and told him that the engineering team set her up, so she fired the one who walked off stage, but then they all quit! Roger, a normally quiet guy, blew a gasket. He told Julianna to get the first plane back and hung up on her. He then spent the rest of the day trying to do damage control by calling the potential buyers and the engineers and sales team, trying to get them all back on board.

Within a twenty-four-hour period, the company had gone from a slow-growing, marginally profitable, not-so-innovative systems and process house to the laughing stock of the industry, missing about fifteen of the best and brightest on their team. Additionally, the state tax audit had exposed that the new AP/AR clerk had not paid the sales taxes for over nine months, not due to malfeasance but to lack of training, resulting in a significant fine, not to mention the back payment. However, malfeasance did show up, thanks to the investments bankers' due diligence. Julianna had been moving money around to hide the fact that she had been "borrowing" from the company for years, to the tune of several million dollars.

Roger sat back and reflected on what he had wanted when he started the company, the mission, the vision, and the values that he had once had. It had all gone up in smoke, and he couldn't figure out how it had happened—slowly and then suddenly. What had he done?

In the following chapters, the Automation Engineers case study will unfold piece by piece to reveal what happens when a company's culture is ignored. It will be used to help emphasize and portray why companies should pay attention to their cultures. The information and lessons surrounding this case study will ensure that you and your company don't end up like Roger and Automation Engineers.

Chapter One

Why Does Culture Matter?

Merriam-Webster defines culture as:

the beliefs, customs, arts, etc., of a particular society, group, place, or time
a particular society that has its own beliefs, ways of life, art, etc.
a way of thinking, behaving, or working that exists in a place or
organization (such as a business)

Culture is always present, whether we like it or not. All groups, societies, and organizations have it. Often, they just don't know it or know how to name it. In some cases, they may not want to believe it is what it is. You might be asking: Since it's already there, why don't we pay more attention to it? The answer for business is often because it's considered one of those "soft" subjects that most entrepreneurs, CEOs, and leaders consider touchy-feely, unimportant, immovable, or just plain uncomfortable. If they say the company has a good culture, that seems to be good enough for most organizations, meaning they intend to have a good culture, but whether they really know what the company's culture is, is doubtful.

However, what is rarely asked is: *Why* is the culture the way it is and *why* does it matter? It matters because successful companies have good cultures—cultures whose values, beliefs, and behaviors are aligned. This is called *intentional culture*. Methodically identifying the values at the core of the organization and translating those into a language that is lived, visible, and measurable inside the organization is key to achieving success. The reverse of this is *unintentional culture*, or the unstated culture that is living and breathing inside an organization that creates chaos and failure.

Let's think about Automation Engineers for a minute. It's pretty obvious that Roger didn't intend for the culture to be what it was, but it was hard-wired for dysfunction. The majority of the stated values—trust, expertise, innovation, winning, customer service, caring, honesty, and integrity—had long been abandoned and replaced by the unintentional or disconnected culture that was present and growing like a cancer. And it started with Roger. Failing to confront his dishonest and bullying COO meant that honesty and trust were just words and not values to be lived in the organization.

In most cases, the barrier to defining intentional culture is getting people to talk about values. There are two reasons for this: first, it makes people uncomfortable, and second, most don't know how to identify their own values, let alone those of the organization. When a CEO is asked about their personal values, the most common replies are almost always *integrity* and *honesty*. This is easy and culturally acceptable to say—who wants to say they don't have these values? But beyond these, the list is almost nonexistent. Having rarely been asked the question, they will default to the values on the wall poster that was created in marketing eons ago by a founder or team other than theirs or, worse, ordered online from some inspirational poster company.

Why culture matters for an organization is that it is often the single biggest reason for success or failure. Cultures are neither good nor bad; they simply are. Some produce results; some do not.

Successful companies have cultures that produce growth and achieve the goals and objectives faster than those with unhealthy or dysfunctional cultures. In companies with good cultures, attracting and retaining talent becomes much easier and cheaper. Your employees become the recruiting arm for the firm. Customer satisfaction is higher because employees are happier and people want to do business with people who are happy. How often have you changed companies after being treated poorly by a customer service person? How many people did you tell? We tend to share our negative experiences far more than our positive ones. Good company culture feeds on itself and produces results; dysfunctional culture create more dysfunction.

A good company culture is defined by "lived" values, but it also needs a compelling mission and vision. However, without the values, mission and vision are a complete waste of time.

Mission is defined as why the company exists—what are you here to accomplish?

- We exist to do X = What

- We do it for Y = Who

- We do it by Z = How

If you craft a couple of sentences that answer the above, you will have a mission, one that sits atop your values.

We are committed to designing and manufacturing the best positional support systems for every wheelchair user. We make it easily adaptable to individual needs and empower every person to achieve their best.

— Mission statement for Bodypoint, a company that manufactures positioning systems for complex rehab patients confined to wheelchairs

Vision is the place you are going, the future you are making. Defining your vision is about looking beyond the constraints you have today and seeing the possibilities of tomorrow. It's what could be but does not yet exist. This is what you get to create. Do you remember this one: "A computer on every desk and in every home"? This was the original vision for Microsoft. What was once considered crazy, impossible, or "why would you want one?" is now considered "was there a time when we didn't?" That was a big vision.

The good news for organizations is that creating an intentional culture is likely one of the least expensive things to help a company grow, yet it is the one that is almost always ignored—both financially and strategically. Create a new marketing campaign! Buy more equipment! Hire the best talent! Find a strategic investment firm to bring in more cash! Build or move to a new location! All can be the right strategy for a company, but all cost a lot of money, which for entrepreneurs is one of the least readily available resources. You will rarely see "Create and Live Our Intentional Culture" on this list. If you did, it would be dismissed or easily overlooked as the best road for growth—or worse, the belief "we already have that, don't we?" If only culture were better understood!

Think about Roger's peers whose companies all passed him up. He started with more money than they did. He took some of the best talent from IBM when he started. In most cases, his products were superior to those of his competitors, so why did they all cross the $100M mark and he couldn't get past $30M? A culture that worked versus one that did not. When your talent abandons you, the best products, strategic plans, or the most money won't matter.

Fortunately for business, Millennials do understand good (functional, successful) company culture. Guess where they choose to spend their time? With those companies. Since this is the workforce of the future, it might be a good idea for companies to spend some time defining and creating their intentional cultures. Consider it the secret weapon and the best value or ROI ever gained on investments directly into the organization.

In 2017 Wells Fargo took quite a beating in stock value and public relations based on several missteps. The frontline tellers, sales reps, and customer service employees were incented to create new accounts. The managers took it a step further and encouraged them to create fake accounts, thereby duping unsuspecting clients into opening new accounts, or in some cases opening new accounts without the clients' knowledge. When the entire scandal was revealed, there was a lot of talk about how the behavior was "against our core values," and they committed to getting rid of anyone behaving this way. Unfortunately for Wells Fargo, the rot went a little deeper than the few managers and 5,000 frontline people they let go. Apparently, the CEO and board knew what was going on, and as the whole cover up unraveled, the CEO and several board members were forced to resign. That might have been the end of the story, but what they neglected to do was really look at the culture (i.e., values) at the root of the problem and address it. Values produced the behavior that got them into trouble. About a year later, surprise, surprise, the insurance department was caught selling insurance policies to people who didn't need them or didn't even know they had them! Sound familiar? Behavior follows beliefs, and beliefs come from values. If the values are not those stated, they are the living, breathing values at the core of a dysfunctional culture. In this case, the faces changed, but the values and culture did not because too many of the people who were rewarded for the behavior stayed.

Another company whose culture was overtaken by some very bad actors was Enron. They had phenomenal growth in the early days and made acquisition after acquisition. They were the darling of Wall Street and almost one of those "too big to fail" companies. Unfortunately, underneath it all, the CFO had been stealing millions of dollars through creative financing. In order to cover the losses, he convinced the CEO to make all the employees invest their 401(k)s in Enron stock only—to show their support and faith in the company. Of course, the scandal eventually unraveled and the CFO and CEO went to jail for fraud. But the real tragedy was that thousands of employees lost all of their savings and pensions, not to mention their jobs. One person's values infected another's, and before anyone knew it, the entire culture had shifted from one of innovation and inspiration to one of greed and deceit.

When I ran my company, I noticed how quickly and efficiently anything could happen when we were all aligned. We were really on fire when we were living our values. It was like all the arrows were going in the same direction. I didn't have words for it at the time, but I always noticed when we won and when we lost. Ever notice how finger-pointing and blame happen when something doesn't work as planned in some organizations, while in others they quickly go to work on what they could have done better? That's the difference between functional cultures and dysfunctional cultures.

I worked with one CEO of a manufacturing group that had significant ups and downs in performance. According to the CEO, his people were unreliable. First, they weren't his people, they were people. Second, there was always enough blame and shame to go around but never praise. When I pointed out that the problem might be with him—and a lack of shared values, vision, and mission—he blamed me for not understanding the problem. I understood it all too well, but he wasn't ready to hear or see it. I stopped working with him after that, and he ended up calling me three months later to say I was right and to see if I was willing to help. My response was: if, and only if, we could start with values and do a cultural reset. He agreed and one year later we had rising profits and an engaged team—and a new CEO that believed in culture. The board also had the same idea that I did.

Had Roger realized that culture was at the root of his company's growth problem, he might have been able to make some changes early on. But once a few people take hold of a toxic culture, it's like *Lord of the Flies*: before you know it, everyone is behaving in ways that cause us to stare wide-eyed in disbelief.

Roger was having to confront the wreckage of his once profitable company, and he wanted to put it back together. But where to start? He had a vague sense that it had something to do with this toxic culture that had been allowed to grow. How had he let this happen?

Rather than spend too much time pondering the question of culture, Roger instead did what he always did, which was to talk it over with Julianna. This was familiar to him; change was not.

Chapter Two

INTENTIONAL CULTURE VS. UNINTENTIONAL CULTURE

Culture is the daily demonstration of a company's values. It can be the manifestation of the stated values or the unstated values, but are nonetheless real values that some or all of the employees share. If a company demonstrates unstated values on a daily basis, that company has an unintentional culture. It's a sad reality that a high percentage of the cultures in organizations today are completely unintentional. At Automation Engineers, Roger did not set out to have a toxic, dishonest culture; he just wanted to make great products with smart people. But over the years the culture was appropriated by Julianna's beliefs, and because she was in a position of unchecked power, that became the unintentional culture.

Mission and vision are a complete waste of time if they are not reinforced daily by the values of the organization. Values are the foundation that hold up the mission and vision. Think about values as the living and breathing heart of the company. If you ignore them, the organism dies—much like mission and vision become afterthoughts if values are not reinforced. In organizations, another organism will always rise to take its place. These will be the alternative values of the person who fundamentally does not share the stated values of the company. This person does not want to be the only one with alternative values or beliefs, and so they actively work to engage others who think like them. No one likes to be unhappy alone; we are much better when we can find others to engage in our unhappiness, and find someone or something to blame. Pretty soon these rogue individuals, or "cultural terrorists," take over and reshape and define the culture in their own image—often referred to as "toxic culture," but really it's only toxic to the stated values. This is how unintentional culture is born. The real values are not reinforced, and a dominant person or group takes over with their own set of values, which are almost always different or opposite of what was intended.

The result is slow or nonexistent growth, and it can often be the difference between success and failure in a company. Aligned, intentional cultures produce better results and achieve their goals faster than unintentional cultures. Attracting and retaining the right talent becomes much easier because it's all in the open. There is nothing to hide, no skeletons in the closet, no explanations for the Julianna-like individuals of the world. Ultimately, all companies want growth. Intentional cultures grow twice as fast as those with unintentional cultures.

When we think about values, it's often something taken for granted, but mostly misunderstood. No one will admit that they do not know what their values are, but few can actually name them. Why it matters is this:

- Values drive beliefs.

- Beliefs drive behaviors.

- Behaviors drive performance.

- Performance drives results.

This is from the work of Simon Sinek, who talks about *why* we do things versus *what* we do. When applied to organizations, the *why* is often referred to as the mission statement—and it often can be—but more often the mission statement is the *what*. Usually the *why* is the values. It's what unites people to come together to achieve something. In aligned, intentional cultures you will see consistent behaviors that achieve results. In companies that have unintentional cultures, like Automation Engineers, you will see a lack of results, or inconsistent performance at best. Think of it like one of those horror movies where the green slime slowly takes over the whole lab and then escapes into the greater world. Unintentional cultures are ugly, they are not fun places to work, and, most importantly, they do not produce results for the owners, shareholders, employees, or vendors.

Think about values as the guardrails of the culture or, as I've also referred to them, as the kiddie bumpers on the bowling alley—you will not get a gutter ball if you adhere to the values. Values will keep everyone in the right lane or right alley and prevent unintentional culture from taking hold. Once values are visible, stated, and lived, it becomes very easy for everyone to understand how to make decisions in the organization.

One of the stated values of an organization I worked with was accountability. They came to me to talk about an employee who refused to be held accountable. He frequently lied about completing his work and caused his coworkers to do his work in order to meet deadlines. He was personable, but they were having a hard time confronting him. I explained what was happening to their culture and how they were negating one of their stated core values by not holding this individual accountable. This was an agency contracted by the government, and if employees weren't let go before their one-year anniversary, it was like an act of Congress to terminate them. The leadership could not agree on pulling the trigger and the dead-line passed. Now, three years later, the organization is in disarray, the good employees have moved on, the ones that remain refuse to work with this guy, and he has manipulated yet another supervisor into giving him another chance. The value of accountability is dead or, worse, a joke to the remaining employees. We are what we tolerate.

Contrast this to Zappos. They are one of those great examples of intentional culture that lives and breathes its values every day. Zappos was founded in 1999 in Las Vegas as an online shoe company by Tony Hsieh, who, by most measures, is a different type of CEO. The company sold to Amazon in 2009 for $1.2 billion, so, different or not, it was incredibly successful. Amazon was smart and pretty much left them alone to sell lots of shoes and throw money to the bottom line. They did not try to change the culture—why mess with a good thing? This was a very astute move on their part.

Zappos has ten principles that they live by, even after the acquisition by Amazon:

1. Deliver wow through service

2. Embrace and drive change

3. Create fun and a little weirdness

4. Be adventurous, creative, and open-minded

5. Pursue growth and learning

6. Build open and honest relationships with communication

7. Build a positive team and family spirit

8. Do more with less

9. Be passionate and determined

10. Be humble

Each of these principles is grounded in a value, and it becomes a road map for how to operate. If there is ever a question as to how to behave, one of these ten principles will tell them exactly what to do. Reportedly, they did things like give new hires two weeks to decide if they wanted to stay at Zappos and would pay them one month's salary if they decided to leave. This is about as honest and open as it gets in determining whether it's a right fit for a new hire. The employees are also completely empowered to "do what's right for the customer": they do not need permission to return items, replace them, or give credit. Their number one principle tells them to "deliver WOW through service," so they do. This has resulted in both empowered workers and very happy customers. Remember, they had to get people to trust that buying shoes online in 1999 was a safe thing to do, so they not only made it safe but they reinforced the customers' decision to try them out with every sale. And they made it fun.

They also have a throne in the front area of the company that each new employee sits on the first day they start—they even get a crown. Then the rest of the employees tell them why it's such a great place to work and take turns describing the values. That seems "fun and a little weird"! The company did take one dip in growth and popularity when Tony Hseih, CEO, decided that he liked the concept of *holacracy*. Essentially this is a flat management structure where there are no managers or management structure. This was a risky change for an organization that was very successful. He began in 2015, and when the rollout was rocky, he lost about twenty percent of employees and managers. He had to step back and determine if holacracy was what he really wanted. It was. He paid generous severances to those who left, aligned with company values, and hoped for the best. Growth and profits took a dip, but he stuck with it. Today, they still use this structure. Growth and profits are still not at the pace they were prior to the shift, but Hsieh is determined that this is how he wants to run things. It fits for him. Losing twenty percent of your workforce is a difficult maneuver for any organization to pull off, and not surprisingly, there were those who were not comfortable in the new culture. Because that's precisely what he did: change culture. Now, those who join the team will know going in what it is and turnover will be much less. When you change things on employees midstream, regardless of the change, it becomes a broken promise and very hard to recover from. Even with the lower performance, Hseih claims his only regret is not doing it sooner.

Microsoft is another company that has had ups and downs based on changing culture inside the organization. On its website, Microsoft lists "what we value," which is an interesting, nuanced take on "our values." Is it how they operate or how they want to be seen?

- Innovation

- Diversity and inclusion

- Corporate social responsibility

- Philanthropies

- Environment

- Trustworthy computing

Its mission says, "We believe in what people make possible. Our mission is to empower every person and every organization on the planet to achieve more."

Each of these values is more about what they do than who they are and how they operate. All are very aspirational, but the reality is somewhat different if you talk with employees—at least on the Redmond campus. The current CEO, Satya Nadella, took over from Steve Ballmer in 2014. One of his goals was to create a more collaborative culture—a significant change from the very siloed culture that had existed. Just to be clear, I don't think Bill Gates, Paul

Allen, or Ballmer set out to create the silos and competitive culture that existed inside the organization. It just happened; it became the unintentional culture. "A Computer on Every Desk and in Every Home" was an amazingly inspiring vision back in the 1980s, but it was not accompanied by a specific set of company values, or at least not any that were reinforced. When unintentional cultures produce success, no one looks too closely at the values. When they stumble, it's the first thing discussed.

Microsoft in its early days was massively successful, primarily driven by the values of the founder—Gates. Although I don't think these values were stated, they were lived. And the result was silos. The silos were then seen as an obstacle to growth, and they were unintentional but not surprising due to the culture that had been lived up until that point.

The silos, or specifically the lack of collaboration, happened because Gates and, subsequently, Ballmer were very competitive and singularly focused guys. Not surprisingly, they hired and promoted very competitive people as the leaders of all the different divisions. Winning and competition were reinforced at all levels, so naturally the divisions competed with one another, creating silos. This culture is still quite evident today. A very talented woman I know went to work there in a high-level marketing position. The rest of the team, many of whom had been there for years, was not helpful or collaborative. The message she quickly got was, "Figure it out yourself; we had to, so you do too. If you make it, we *might* work with you, but don't count on it." It's very much an "everyone for themselves" mentality, which reinforces the silo mentality and complete lack of collaboration.

In the early days of the late 1980s and early '90s, the stories around Seattle were all about the brutal hiring interviews that lasted most of the day. The engineers were given difficult, if not impossible, scenarios to code or figure out. The pressure was high, and those doing the interviewing were gleeful now that the shoe was on the other foot, constantly making it harder to get in than when they had to go through it. It became more like hazing than interviewing. It reinforced the unspoken value of fierce competition.

While I believe the current CEO, Nadella, is very well intentioned and collaboration is exactly what they need to create a much more robust growth trajectory, it will be a heavy lift, if not an impossible task, if some of the old guard is not shown the door and their new values rolled out with actual programs, behaviors, and rewards associated with them. The competitive, non-collaborative environment set up in the early days produced amazing results because they did not have a lot of competition, and the sheer mass of innovation and drive kept things growing. However, to maintain the growth demanded by investors, a shift is needed to a collaborative culture that does not eat its own, and thus produces an unintentional culture.

Intentional culture like Zappos's is easier to achieve when you start the company with very present and specific values. Unintentional culture takes a hard root, as in the Microsoft case, when everyone just keeps reinforcing the behaviors and values that have always existed but are unstated.

Is your company's culture intentional or unintentional? If you are not achieving your goals, I'll go out on a limb here and say it's one hundred percent unintentional. I'm sure it's not what you wanted or thought you would get when you started the company. What likely happened is that your values were ill defined, unstated, or not reinforced, so the unintentional culture had a chance to rise in the chasm where the values should have been. It was invisible, except for the annoyance of bad actors and lack of performance as a whole.

Similarly, Roger was blind to what was happening right in front of him; he couldn't connect the dots. He didn't have a dishonest bone in his body, but his inability to see, let alone confront, Julianna's dishonest behavior allowed her values to become the company's, and unintentional culture took root. Much like an invasive species of plant or animal that takes over, unintentional culture is a survivor.

Roger's investors had backed out, Julianna was begging for forgiveness, and Roger had convinced about eight of the employees who quit at the tradeshow to come back to work—for more money, of course, which was now a huge problem, as the back taxes had taken a big chunk of the company reserves. Julianna had convinced him that her "moving" money from accounts was not intentional; she thought she was making "investments" for the company and would of course give the money back if Roger wasn't happy with her choices. Roger again chose to ignore this particular problem.

The other massive problem was the hit to the company's reputation. How could they possibly come back from this epic failure at the trade show? He had always prided himself on the superiority and innovation of their products, but he was now an industry joke. He was tired and he wanted out, but his options were becoming more limited by the day.

Roger didn't need the money—he had plenty and he had never cared much for material things. What he did want, however, was his reputation back. How had he let things get so out of touch? He needed to rethink a short-term vision. He wanted to be innovative and the expert again. He just wasn't sure he could do it by himself.

Chapter Three

How to Identify Your Values

Values are the deeply ingrained beliefs that drive behaviors. As we look to identify our own values, both business and personal, some important clues lie in the stories of our lives. We develop our values early on, mostly unconsciously, but they become our way of navigating the world. Children are for the most part blank slates, and the core values they develop usually depend upon the environments they grow up in. If you were raised in a household that was religious, service oriented, agnostic, latchkey, political, kind, harsh, controlling, free-spirited, competitive, supportive, or any one of thousands of adjectives we use to describe values, you were exposed to these values. You either made the choice to embrace the values at the core of these beliefs, or you adopted some of your own.

The first way to identify your own values is to think about some of the pivotal stories you remember from your childhood or early life. What is the first story you think of? How old were you? What was your takeaway or lesson from that event? At the core of that story, did the value you adopt shape the way you viewed the world from that point on?

When I was sixteen I had one of those key, value-shaping experiences. Shortly before returning from a year as an exchange student in Costa Rica, I learned that my father had abandoned our family of seven children. This alone was a terrible shock, for what I believed was a very close Catholic family, but I also learned that we had no money because my dad took it all with him. As the oldest daughter, I arrived home to find my home very different from when I had left. Suddenly, my mom was working and in a complete daze, we were on welfare, the church was leaving food baskets on our doorstep, and my brothers and sisters were, to put it mildly, confused.

On top of all this, I discovered that, in my absence, the room I had shared had been given to another sibling and my few belongings had been passed on to my sisters. I was told I would have a room that used to belong to my younger brothers. You can imagine what it looked like. In a big family, having something all your own is a rarity. Losing all of what had been mine, the life I knew, at once, hit hard.

After I had been home about a week, my grandfather came to visit. He was a quiet man and looked a lot like Jimmy Stewart. Looking around my room, he said, "This doesn't look like you. Would you like to change it?" Of course I said yes, so my grandfather took me to a store where we picked out wallpaper and paint. For the next week, he showed me how to transform my unwanted room into something beautiful. But more important than regaining a sense of space was the quiet wisdom my grandfather imparted to me as we worked. He never said anything more negative about my father than, "I don't understand how a man can abandon his family." But he followed that with a key value that has become part of who I am: "It's important to always do the right thing, no matter the cost." The room my grandfather helped me make was wonderful, but the real gift was the lasting lesson of honor, integrity, and authenticity he taught me. This became my story.

Two other ways to identify your core values are what Dave Logan, author of *Tribal Leadership*, calls "hell no" and "high five" moments. "Hell no" moments are those in which you absolutely refuse to do something or let something happen. When someone asks you to cross a line, lie, or do something unethical, even if it's for a good cause, would you do it? The point at which you said no was a value you would not cross, a bridge too far, as they say. When a whistleblower reports wrongdoing, even with much peril to themselves, they are standing up for their values. When you protect someone from being bullied, you are staking a claim on your values set. The marches in our nation's capital for civil rights, war protests, women's rights, and most recently for gun control are all examples of "hell no" moments. The protesters are saying "hell no" to what for them is a crossing over of a value or deeply held belief.

"High five" moments are those that we celebrate. They can be winning a race of some sort, graduating first in your class, accomplishing a goal, sailing around the world, or really anything that you deem worthy of celebration. In that celebration, at its core, is a value you are celebrating. My youngest sister, Ami, was diagnosed with MS when she was thirty-five years old. She had always been a marathoner and very active, so this was a big blow to her. However, she decided she was not going to let it get in the way of her running an Ironman. She trained for a year and felt she was ready, despite her right leg which "drops," or becomes inoperable when she gets very tired or hot. We all went to Coeur D'Alene to watch her complete the course. She made it through the swimming portion in good time in spite of unseasonably cold weather. The 112 miles of biking was a little slower than she had wanted, but she still felt she was on pace to finish in the seventeen hours it takes to qualify to say you have completed it. She was not going for speed, just going for a finish.

Both of her training partners finished in just over ten hours. She completed the first half of the 26.22-mile run pretty well, with a combination of walking and running, but her leg was dropping a lot, so her progress was significantly slowing. When she passed the halfway mark of the run, they told her she was twenty minutes shy of the requirement to qualify so she was out. She was devastated, not to mention tired, hot, and crying, and it was dark. I think the average person would have called it good and quit, but not Ami; she hunkered down and kept going. At 12:20 a.m. she crossed a finish line we had made in front of the house we were all staying at that was half a mile from the actual finish line, which was closed. We banged pots and pans and made her break the ribbon. She was ecstatic! Her leg had ceased to work so she was dragging it along, using her arm to help pull it up with each step. She showed such an immense amount of perseverance that we were all moved to tears. Perseverance—a value that she has shown throughout her life. This was a high five for all of us watching as well.

A founder will often adapt his or her personal values as those of the business without really giving it too much thought. There is an assumption that this is how the world operates. In this case, it's easy for the founder or owner to be deeply aligned with those values because they are their personal values as well; they know and own them. It becomes easy to explain and easy to live.

Where it becomes much more difficult to navigate is when employees join an organization that already has its values established. How do we know this company shares *our* values? Or, more importantly, lives them? Even more problematic is an organization that hires a new CEO who says he or she shares the values that the company was founded on but does not.

A values exercise with an organization looks something like this: Gather the leaders or managers in a room, or the whole company if it's small enough, and have someone facilitate gathering all the values that the participants can think of. You will need poster-size flip charts and will likely end up with fifty to one hundred value words. Then you begin the process of eliminating those that seem like duplicates or just don't apply to this group. You keep doing this exercise until you end up with ten to fifteen. Then the hard part really starts. Trying to get an existing group to agree on three to seven values is hard. People will stake out their opinions and dig in. The key lies in the definition for each of the words. For example, *collaboration* can mean many different things to different people, so this is where you will get into more detail about the meaning versus just the word. The reason you don't want more than seven is you won't remember them.

This is not a wordsmithing exercise. This is about creating meaningful values for yourself and/or your organization that people will embrace and live. These are the guardrails for behavior. Once you have determined what you *think* they are, you need to wear them for two to four months to see if they really are your values, and if you got the definition right, or if maybe two fit into one. An existing organization has these already, stated or unstated. The leader's job is to get them on paper and see if they're what you really want.

Creativity | Impact | Caring | Curiosity | Authenticity | Integrity
Honesty | Empathy | Execution | Fun | Respect| Love
Confidentiality |Diligence | Excellence | Innovation
Collaboration | Achievement | Teamwork | Trust | Expert | Fierce
Leadership | Inclusive | Communication | Adaptability
Analytical | Focus | Drive | Competitive | Growth | Success
Courage | Contribution | Challenge | Passion

These are just a few of the thousands of words that could be considered values. Remember, there are no good or bad values, only those that work for you and your organization or not. Some produce better outcomes than others and some may be considered amoral, but they are still values that people hold. An unchangeable behavior is usually tied to a long-held belief that is a core value—and people rarely if ever change their core values.

Let's take a look at an organization that does a great job of defining its values and definitions. Amazon, founded in 1994 by Jeff Bezos, is now the second-largest private employer in the US. They have what they call "Leadership Principles," which they say define their culture, and, as I believe, define their values.

Leadership Principles

Our Leadership Principles define Amazon's culture. They aren't just a pretty inspirational wall hanging. Amazonians use them every day, whether they're discussing ideas for new projects, deciding on the best solution for a customer's problem, or interviewing candidates.

Customer Obsession

Leaders start with the customer and work backwards. They work vigorously to earn and keep customer trust. Although leaders pay attention to competitors, they obsess over customers.

Ownership

Leaders are owners. They think long term and don't sacrifice long-term value for short-term results. They act on behalf of the entire company, beyond just their own team. They never say "that's not my job."

Invent and Simplify

Leaders expect and require innovation and invention from their teams and always find ways to simplify. They are externally aware, look for new ideas everywhere, and are not limited by "not invented here." As we do new things, we accept that we may be misunderstood for long periods of time.

Are Right, A Lot

Leaders are right a lot. They have strong judgment and good instincts. They seek diverse perspectives and work to disconfirm their beliefs.

Learn and Be Curious

Leaders are never done learning and always seek to improve themselves. They are curious about new possibilities and act to explore them.

Hire and Develop the Best

Leaders raise the performance bar with every hire and promotion. They recognize exceptional talent, and willingly move them throughout the organization. Leaders develop leaders and take seriously their role in coaching others. We work on behalf of our people to invent mechanisms for development like Career Choice.

Insist on the Highest Standards

Leaders have relentlessly high standards—many people may think these standards are unreasonably high. Leaders are continually raising the bar and drive their teams to deliver high-quality products, services, and processes. Leaders ensure that defects do not get sent down the line and that problems are fixed so they stay fixed.

Think Big

Thinking small is a self-fulfilling prophecy. Leaders create and communicate a bold direction that inspires results. They think differently and look around corners for ways to serve customers.

Bias for Action

Speed matters in business. Many decisions and actions are reversible and do not need extensive study. We value calculated risk-taking.

Frugality

Accomplish more with less. Constraints breed resourcefulness, self-sufficiency and invention. There are no extra points for growing headcount, budget size, or fixed expense.

Earn Trust

Leaders listen attentively, speak candidly, and treat others respectfully. They are vocally self-critical, even when doing so is awkward or embarrassing. Leaders do not believe their or their team's body odor smells of perfume. They benchmark themselves and their teams against the best.

Dive Deep
Leaders operate at all levels, stay connected to the details, audit frequently, and are skeptical when metrics and anecdote differ. No task is beneath them.

Have Backbone; Disagree and Commit
Leaders are obligated to respectfully challenge decisions when they disagree, even when doing so is uncomfortable or exhausting. Leaders have conviction and are tenacious. They do not compromise for the sake of social cohesion. Once a decision is determined, they commit wholly.

Deliver Results
Leaders focus on the key inputs for their business and deliver them with the right quality and in a timely fashion. Despite setbacks, they rise to the occasion and never settle.

These fourteen leadership principles drive the company's behavior, internally and externally, to create the very successful company that it is today. For the most part, it has worked spectacularly well. However, they did hit a significant speed bump when a NYT investigative piece in August of 2015 described the brutal culture inside Amazon. A lot of it was widely known, especially here in Seattle. The employees, or Amazonians, were willing to put up with long hours, ridiculous work schedules and deadlines, and harsh, bullying treatment all because they were a part of building something amazing and they could leverage the experience as a stepping stone. What was not as widely known was the back channel that all employees had to complain about or rat out an incompetent person or someone they just didn't agree with. This fostered a level of distrust and backbiting that was creating a toxic environment, threatening to destroy the successful culture that had been built.

Remember that principle (value) to "Earn Trust"? "Leaders listen attentively, speak candidly, and treat others respectfully. They are vocally self-critical, even when doing so is awkward or embarrassing. Leaders do not believe their or their team's body odor smells of perfume. They benchmark themselves and their teams against the best." By setting up a back channel, they were violating this value. They were not vocally self-critical; they were secretly critical of others. Bezos is known for his need for data, data, data. Back in the late '90s, I heard Andy Grove, the former CEO of Intel, speak and when asked about Amazon he was very prescient in saying that its value was not an online bookstore; its value was the data and buying habits the company was amassing to sell to people in a brand-new way. I distinctly remember that the majority of the room did not believe him. He was *so* very right on. In this need for data, someone decided that creating this back channel to gather data on the team was a great idea. It fundamentally violated the "Earn Trust" value, and the culture was tripped up, or unintentional, until they remedied it.

What are your stories? Your organization's stories? The high fives and hell nos that guide your behavior? Ask yourself what core value is at the root of that belief. It's yours to protect and to live.

Let's go back to Automation Engineers and think about their values. Remember, at one point they had posted the following values on the wall: trust, expertise, innovation, winning, customer service, caring, honesty, integrity. Interestingly, if you look at their current website, they don't list any of these. If we look at what's happening inside the organization, they are behaving in direct conflict with caring, honesty, integrity, and trust. Speed has replaced the desire for innovation, and winning seems to mean only when Juliana says it's winning. Unintentional culture has taken over. How do they get it back? Roger was not taking a leadership position on it and began to spend more and more time away since the infamous trade show incident.

The lead engineer, Jack, decided that the only way to dissolve the unintentional culture was to get Julianna out of the company. He determined that she was the sole reason it was all falling apart, that the company was good but that she, and she alone, was the problem. People loved the technology and the freedom to create things, but she was stifling all the creativity. He decided that he and the lead sales engineer who quit could make a bid to buy the company. They got some backers and put together a decent offer for Roger. It's not clear what Roger actually thought of the offer, or if he even got it, because he never responded directly to them. Instead, Julianna sent out a company-wide email stating emphatically that Roger would not consider such an insulting offer from said employees, especially since one was no longer with the company. She stated flatly that she and Roger would take the company to new heights with their combined leadership.

This was the last straw for the engineer. He tendered his resignation, and he and the sales engineer decided to take their financial backers and create a competing company to Automation Engineers. They started creating the business plan with their values: innovation, expertise, trust, collaboration, and respect.

Chapter Four

Owning the Values in Your Business

In order to make sure that the stated values of the company, or the intentional culture, is not lost as soon as the ink is dry, the values must be reflected on a daily basis. This lesson was taught to me a long time ago by a speaker for Vistage who was coming to speak to one of my groups. The company hosting the meeting was a software company specializing in memory devices. The employees were primarily scientists, software engineers, and project managers. As I was leading the speaker through the cubicles to the "conference room" (which was really just a back room with some folding tables set up), he asked me to stop. He said, "Look around this office." Granted, it was a mess, with papers and stuff strewn around everywhere and just general disorder, but I wasn't sure what he wanted me to see. It turned out to be exactly that. "Take a look at this mess; it says everything about them as a company. I bet they never deliver things on time," he remarked. He was exactly right—that was the biggest problem in this company and the thing that had prevented them from winning the bigger deals and becoming the subject of an acquisition, which they really wanted.

How your company looks and feels is a reflection of what values you stand for and who you are as an organization. From that first walk-through, I was keenly aware of what showed up when I visited businesses. It was either a validation of their stated values or a reflection of what the company really valued—likely the unintentional culture. In the example of the software company, the engineers liked to tinker but hated to be held accountable. One of their stated values was "fun." For them, playing every day without really worrying about getting anything finished was fun. If they actually did manage to finish something, they kept tinkering anyway because, again, it was fun. This would not likely be the definition of fun for most of us, but for them it was, all stemming from the owner's need to have work be fun. He surrounded himself with those who felt the same way he did. The only problem with this is it's not a viable business. Without accountability, it's just an adult play space, and at some point the money will run out. Which for the software company was exactly what happened—and it definitely wasn't fun.

Your values are reflected in everything about your company, stated or not stated. They should be visible in:

- The look and feel of the office or location: What does this reflect, intentionally or unintentionally?

- Hiring practices: Do you hire based on values?

- Celebrations: Do we have any awards or celebrations based on our values?

- Compensation/reward structures: Are these consistent with who we are?

- Sales process: If we value the customer, is our sales process reflective of that?

- Marketing: How are we marketing ourselves? Are we hiding or showcasing our real values?

- Strategic planning process: Is it consistent with who we are?

- Customer engagement practices: Are we looking for customers aligned with our values?

The reason you need to keep the values visible in all you do is that it will reinforce DAILY what you stand for. It becomes a reminder and guide to how the company operates. If there is ever a question, they should only need to take a look at the values—and daily behavior—to know how to answer.

A small medical service company that I visited was having staffing challenges, so I went to meet with the CEO. When I arrived, no one was at the front desk to greet me, although I could hear voices behind. I waited approximately ten minutes, but no one came out to meet me. I finally noticed a phone on the desk in the waiting area with a tiny sign that said, "Call your party," so I picked up the phone but had no idea what extension to dial, as he had not given me one. I just randomly called one and got an answer. I explained I was there to see the CEO. After a long wait, the person explained that the CEO was not there, and asked if I could wait. I waited and another ten minutes later a guy came out to tell me the CEO was hung up in another meeting and I would need to reschedule. I agreed and told him to have him get a hold of me, knowing he would not. He had reached out to me originally, not the other way around.

The values and mission statement were hung in the lobby. Customer service, excellence, respect, and efficiency were their values. "Dedicated to efficient service delivery for all our clients" was the mission statement. Clearly something had gone way off course from the creation of those to what I experienced at their office. I'm sure their customers and employees alike experienced the same disrespect and lack of customer service that I did. It was not a surprise the company was having the challenges it was. No one wants to work for a company that is obviously so out of alignment with its stated values.

Making values real is critical. Defining them so everyone knows the meaning is even more important. If the software company had defined *fun* as "lack of accountability," then they may have made some course corrections early on or realized that by its very definition their success was doomed. If one of your values is in fact "fun," make sure you have *fun*—and a picnic once a year is not considered fun by ninety-nine percent of the working population.

If excellence is one of your values, don't be cheap or accept half measures. This was one of Automation Engineers' challenges. They (Julianna) routinely chose vendors based on low price rather than quality, and the resulting products were not excellent; they were cheap. Remodels were done with subpar materials, and things were always needing repair. One vendor, who everyone thought had been doing terrible press releases, had actually died, and her daughter was carrying on the business but hadn't raised her prices in over ten years so as not to draw attention to herself! Julianna was only interested in the fact that the price had not been raised; she ignored the fact that they were poorly written and rarely picked up by the trade publications.

Marketing is the first place to make sure your values shine through. It's a story worth telling, and good marketing can help people understand who you are and what you stand for. If not, you're just one of many. Customers will choose to do business with you based on relationships, and at the basis of those relationships are your values. When creating your brand and marketing yourself, you will want to showcase your values so that those who would be inclined to do business with companies whose values they respect, or are similar, can spot you easily. Be the green apple in the red barrel.

One Canadian company that does a good job of highlighting their values is AtlasCare. Every year they put out an actual "Culture

Book."Their values are stated on the first few pages along with their mission and vision. Their values are passion, enthusiasm, respect, continuous learning, excellence, and trustworthy. It's about sixty to seventy pages highlighting their people, their accomplishments, their customers, and how all connect to their values. It's fun and makes you want to smile. Every person who works there is in the book and everyone is celebrated. They make enough copies for all of their people and send one to all of their customers. There is no doubt they live their values, every day.

Another company that has been owning its values daily since it started in 1997, and has decimated most of its competition, is Netflix. The original co-founder Reed Hastings is still CEO, and in 2017 they had $11,692 billion in revenue. They entered a crowded field, had a new idea for delivery, and created a whole new industry. They gained recognition early on for the way they hired based on values.

Here is what they list as their values and how they use them on the recruiting page of their website:

Real Values

Many companies have value statements, but often these written values are vague and ignored. The real values of a firm are shown by who gets rewarded or let go. Below are our real values, the specific behaviors and skills we care about most. The more these sound like you, and describe people you want to work with, the more likely you will thrive at Netflix.

Judgment

- You make wise decisions despite ambiguity.

- You identify root causes and get beyond treating symptoms.

- You think strategically and can articulate what you are, and are not, trying to do.

- You are good at using data to inform your intuition.

- You make decisions based on the long term, not near term.

Communication

- You are concise and articulate in speech and writing.

- You listen well and seek to understand before reacting.

- You maintain calm poise in stressful situations to draw out the clearest thinking.

- You adapt your communication style to work well with people from around the world who may not share your native language.

- You provide candid, timely feedback to colleagues.

Curiosity

- You learn rapidly and eagerly.

- You contribute effectively outside of your specialty.

- You make connections that others miss.

- You seek to understand our members around the world and how we entertain them.

- You seek alternate perspectives.

Courage

- You say what you think when it's in the best interest of Netflix, even if it is uncomfortable.

- You are willing to be critical of the status quo.

- You make tough decisions without agonizing.

- You take smart risks and are open to possible failure.

- You question actions inconsistent with our values.

- You are able to be vulnerable in search of truth.

Passion

- You inspire others with your thirst for excellence.

- You care intensely about our members and Netflix's success.

- You are tenacious and optimistic.

- You are quietly confident and openly humble.

Selflessness

- You seek what is best for Netflix, rather than what is best for yourself or your group.

- You are open-minded in search of the best ideas.

- You make time to help colleagues.

- You share information openly and proactively.

Innovation

- You create new ideas that prove useful.

- You re-conceptualize issues to discover solutions to hard problems.

- You challenge prevailing assumptions and suggest better approaches.

- You keep us nimble by minimizing complexity and finding time to simplify.

- You thrive on change.

Inclusion

- You collaborate effectively with people of diverse backgrounds and cultures.

- You nurture and embrace differing perspectives to make better decisions.

- You focus on talent and our values, rather than a person's similarity to yourself.

- You are curious about how our different backgrounds affect us at work, rather than pretending they don't affect us.

- You recognize we all have biases, and work to grow past them.

- You intervene if someone else is being marginalized.

Integrity

- You are known for candor, authenticity, transparency, and being non-political.

- You only say things about fellow employees that you say to their face.

- You admit mistakes freely and openly.

- You treat people with respect independent of their status or disagreement with you.

Impact

- You accomplish amazing amounts of important work.

- You demonstrate consistently strong performance so colleagues can rely upon you.

- You make your colleagues better.

- You focus on results over process.

In addition to using the values as a screening tool for hiring, much like Zappos does, they use their values for employee reviews. Each employee is evaluated on how they adhere to the values, which is a powerful reinforcement for how one should behave. Their values system was put into place back when video stores were still around. I think there is an obvious connection between their values system and their success—*owning and reflecting their values daily.*

Take a look around and see what you are or are not doing to reinforce your values. It will make your job so much easier if you are consistent, and it will help you achieve your goals. These become the kiddie bumpers to make sure you don't get a gutter ball when it comes to culture. No one has to ask what to do or how to do the right thing because it is reinforced in your daily, lived values. It's like hitting the easy button for culture.

Speaking of not having an easy button, things over at Automation Engineers have gone from bad to worse. Roger was furious that Julianna had responded for him and that he hadn't even seen the offer made by the engineer and sales head. But as was Roger's way, he could not confront anyone, least of all Julianna. As we said, all the investors had backed out, and although the offer from the employees was less than Roger thought it was worth, it was his ticket out.

He decided he would reach out to the engineer who quit and see if he could reach a deal. Jack was willing to talk with him, but said that he could no longer work at a place that was ran by someone like Julianna. He could not trust her and did not feel any respect from her, let alone any collaboration. She had a habit of going for "quick wins," which was completely counter to the expertise that was required for their projects. Julianna had completely hijacked whatever culture had been there and over the years made it a reflection of herself. Everything she did was cheap or on the cheap, like the outsourced vendors that were only selected by price. Then manufacturing had to compensate to minimize returned products, costing more in the end, but it didn't matter. Jack vented to Roger, and Roger just nodded in agreement. It was hard to tell if he knew these things or if he was hearing them for the first time.

Roger agreed to take the offer but insisted that Julianna retain her position. Jack refused, so Roger reluctantly agreed to sell to them anyway and said he would have the attorneys begin working on the deal. Jack had known Roger for a long time and trusted that his word was good. He and Scott, the sales engineer, were ecstatic. They would be able to recreate the company with their own values and their own plan. Finally, they could live their values, the ones they thought the company originally stood for. So why did he have this bad feeling?

Chapter Five

HIRING FOR VALUES AND CULTURAL FIT

Reinforcing your company's culture starts with hiring. It's the most obvious and easiest way to find people who will embrace the company's culture. However, hiring for values can be tricky. Even the best interviewers will tell you that hiring is difficult and not an exact science. Nevertheless, hiring for values will exponentially increase the odds that you will make a good hire that fits your culture. Not only will this reinforce your existing culture, it will also save the company time and money.

A bad hire costs the organization a minimum of three times the annual salary of the person. The salary paid, the time lost, the damage to the organization, and all the incidental costs of having to go through the process again are enormous. On top of that, the psychological costs to the company are often higher and more damaging than the actual dollars. A bad cultural hire will make everyone in the organization question if your values really mean anything. And like a virus, a person who doesn't share the values will infect the whole organization in a very short period of time. People want to be around others like them, and a cultural misfit is no different;

they will seek out others like them or try to change people to their point of view. They do this very subtly at first: "funny" comments in the break room, snarky emails to one another, snide side comments in meetings, or jokes about management. They need a partner to engage in the conversation, and once they have gained a confidante, it's easier to find a few more.

"Hire slowly and fire quickly" is a phrase often used by management trainers. This is exactly how hiring should be done. However, it's almost always the opposite that takes place. I have participated in hundreds of interviews over the years, and I think the reason we do it wrong is that, when sitting down face to face with someone, human nature says we want to like them. We are notoriously bad at being neutral and dispassionate enough to ask the really hard questions. Additionally, we want speed. It's usually a crisis that informs us of the need to hire quickly, as if our business will cease to exist if we don't have the position filled immediately. But it's a myth, pure and simple.

In some cases, we have just fired someone, so, really, was this person performing? Were we getting what we needed? The answer is no and we let that go on forever, so why the urgency now? I have never, ever had someone say they wished they had given the person more time after they fired them. It's almost always true that they say, "Why didn't I do this sooner?" And then you find out all the things this person was doing wrong or not doing at all. So the reality is, you have time to find the right person; you don't have time to keep a poor performer on. The old saying "Why do we always have enough time to do it over but never enough to do it right the first time?" certainly applies here.

If someone is leaving of their own accord, we also have time to hire slowly. The rest of the team will step up to the plate to fill in *if*, and only if, you are going to hire the right person for them to work with. First, we want to evaluate that the job is still what it was when we hired the person, and second, we want to figure out *who* the best person for the job will be. If you hire for character, you can train for skills. Of course, you will have the required set of education and experience before you even interview, but you are primarily looking for the right cultural fit, not the perfect résumé match.

Occasionally, you will have someone who is a cultural misfit for the organization but has that one very rare or hard to find talent or skill you really need. This is a slippery slope. There is often a justification by leadership or the manager to hire them because they need that skill so badly, but it's risky. One exception employers make is to have the person work from home, not affecting the workplace culture. However, they will likely interact with others, thereby affecting the culture. Another option I've seen is to hire them as a contractor, which sometimes allows you to have a trial period in order to get a feel for how disruptive they would be to the culture. Neither of these options really works for the long term if their values aren't a fit. Just remember, if you ignore an obvious misfit to your culture, in service to a particular job skill you really need, they will affect the culture. And usually not in a good way.

It is also occasionally possible to show a cultural misfit how a value driving a negative behavior is not serving them. If they have lived a sheltered work life, have never been given feedback, or no one has ever told them how their behavior was affecting their coworkers or their chances for advancement, it might be possible to change their negative behavior. If it's a value that is not deeply held by them but merely adopted out of convenience and lack of feedback, they might be willing to change. You will know because you will see a lasting behavior change. If they resist or are defensive at all or say, "I'll try," it's likely the value is deeply held and not likely to change.

The first step is to develop specific behavioral questions around your values, as Netflix does in its statements about what the behavior looks like associated with each value. Behavior-based questions are always about *past* performance, specific things that have happened, not how someone would behave in the future. People fib about what they might do in the future because often they don't know, so they will tell you what they think you want to know. *You don't care what they might do!* You want to know what they *have* done. This is your best predictor of future behavior. Past performance predicts future behavior.

How to Create Values-Based Interview Questions:

First, start with the stated values. A local company has the following values listed on their website:

- Honesty and integrity

- Respect

- Teamwork

- Excellence

- Fun

Here are a few examples of questions they might use in interviewing for a cultural fit:

Honesty and Integrity

- Discuss a time when your integrity was challenged; how did you handle it?

- Tell me about a time when you experienced a loss for doing what was right; how did you handle it?

- Tell me about a business situation when you felt honesty was inappropriate; why?

Respect

- Give me an example of a time when you felt disrespected; what happened?

- Who deserves respect in an organization and why?

- Tell me about a time when you felt you were respectful to someone but they didn't feel that way.

Teamwork

- Describe a situation when others disagreed with your ideas; what did you do?

- Describe a time when you had to compromise or encourage others to compromise; what was your role? How did you resolve it?

- What was the biggest mistake you have made when delegating work as a part of a team project?

Excellence

- Give me an example of a project that delivered excellent results; what were those?

- Tell me about a time when you were required to produce the highest quality work you have ever done; how did you go about it?

- Have you ever had a time when you had to decide between "good enough" and "excellent" work? How did you handle it?

Fun

- What have you done to celebrate?

- What was the most fun you have ever had on a work project? Why?

- Tell me about a time when you were definitely not having fun even though that was the purpose of the party or exercise.

All of the above questions will encourage the person to think back to situations that seem to be what you are asking for and answer with what they have done. If they have not done it or have a different interpretation of a value than you do, it will come out, naturally.

The worst thing we do when interviewing someone is lead the witness, offering up the answers to them in the form of a question.

- Do you think it would be fun to work here?

- We value teamwork at our organization; how do you feel about it?

- We pride ourselves on excellent work, such as _____ (give a glowing example). Is that what you would consider excellence?

A skilled candidate will tell you exactly what you want to hear because you fed them the right answer in the form of a question, and they will be seamless about it. Even if the candidate is not skilled but is listening at all, they will know how you want them to answer, all without giving specific examples, making their potential behavior hypothetical. You might get lucky and they do believe in those values, but more often than not, they just want to get the job. It's often the best you will ever see them, because they are acting. They are acting like the person you want in order to get the job. They are performing for you. Past behavior will tell you more about who they are than what they "think" about one of your leading, hypothetical questions.

I have also found that asking someone what their values are will be met with momentary confusion, then stuttering, then "honesty, integrity, hard work, and fairness," or some similar bland, generic set of values. I usually follow up by asking for a definition of each of those and am usually met by a blank stare. When you find a person who has identified their personal values and explained them well, you will know they are sincere because they speak from the heart and are passionate about it. But sometimes you will find the person who has done their homework and researched your values and will parrot those back to you. Again, if they are sincere, they will tell you *why*, and you can ask the behavior-based interview questions to verify their truthfulness.

When interviewing, you will only have time to get through five or six of the questions, but it will be enough to give you an idea of who this person is.

The hiring process starts with a concise job description. I usually try to keep it to one page: a succinct paragraph about the responsibilities of the job; a section for required competencies, experience, etc.; and then a section for desired competencies and skills. Once you have this, screen for required competencies and rank by desire, and then create a few values-based interview questions.

Once you've done a phone screen to see if the person meets the basic requirements, you're ready for the interview. I always start by having the person walk me through their résumé, from the first job to the present situation. What I'm listening for are the transitions—why did they leave, what did they like and dislike, etc. This will tell you a lot about who they are and their character if you are listening carefully. Then I ask a few values-based questions and really drill down on each. "Tell me more" is something I say a lot. I'm careful not to share my own stories or what the company is like, because I'm listening for sincerity, not mastery at interviewing. I'm listening for a values fit, things that tell me this person could be successful at the company based on who they are.

The Interview

- 2–3 times

- 2–3 different people or teams (same set of questions)

- 2–3 different places

- Ask what their 60–90 day goals and expectations are.

One reason you want to do multiple interviews—at least two—is that people can fool you. However, it's hard to fib exactly the same way twice, so by having teams or different people interview but asking the same behavior-based values questions, you will get a sense of the person's sincerity. Another reason for multistage interviews is that, with each interview, you learn more about them, more nuance. They reveal a little more as they become more comfortable, and you're trying to get a sense for the real person, their true values, not what they think you want to hear. Also, some of the best people interview terribly. Giving them an opportunity to get to know you, and you them, allows for less nervousness and an ability to really see who they are. Personally, I like to evaluate their manner, dress, timeliness, and eating habits (if it's a position that will host clients), so multiple interviews will give you several times to observe their behavior. Hiring for values is the most important step in guarding against a cultural misfit.

A cultural misfit is a cancer in an organization. Julianna is a perfect example. It's hard to tell what her real values are, but it's evident that she does not embrace the values that Roger started Automation Engineers with.

Trust: She doesn't trust anyone but herself and Roger.

Expertise: She refuses to value quality and forces everyone to do things on the cheap.

Innovation: She values speed over innovation every day and can't wait for things to be developed.

Winning: As long as it's her doing the winning, she's okay with this one.

Customer Service: What? She never speaks to the clients, and throws employees and customers under the bus when it suits her.

Caring: Only for Roger.

Honesty and Integrity: Enough said.

Unfortunately, what has happened over time is that Roger has also abandoned his values and those of the company due to his refusal to confront the cultural misfit. It's like that old horror movie *The Fly* with Jeff Goldblum where he slowly morphs from a man to a fly: at some point, you don't recognize your old self. Not owning your values will do that to you.

I had a sales person once who was very knowledgeable and good at what she did but was completely a loner. She would refuse to participate with the service team and get frustrated by people who didn't do things her way, and was generally unpleasant to be around. The customers liked her because she did take care of them, so it was a perplexing situation. We had an offsite meeting with the sales team and had someone facilitate a values exercise for us, and it became painfully obvious what our problem was. After we had sorted the values down to ten, we could not gain agreement on a lower number.

The one that she refused to agree to was collaboration. She didn't see why it was necessary and would not agree that it should be one of the team's top values, even though the irony of creating values as a team would be considered collaboration. She was much more vocal than the seven other sales people, and surprisingly, they were willing to abandon it. At this point I stepped in and said no. We had always been successful because of our collaborative effort toward problem-solving for the customer and the variety of products we had. I said it was okay that she didn't believe it, but we were adopting it and moving on.

What I knew in that moment was that she was a cultural misfit. Collaboration was core to how we did business, and it was not something she valued. She was a very good individual contributor but not a good team player. After our retreat, I had a conversation with her and said that it didn't seem like this was a good place for her. She agreed and we worked on an exit plan. Her values were not wrong; they were just not a fit for our company. Once she was gone, the collaboration in and between our sales and service team increased exponentially. She was quietly but forcefully holding collaboration back and unconsciously attempting to change the culture to align with her values.

The last phase of hiring for culture is your onboarding process. Other than your interview process, this is the first time they will experience your company's culture. You want to make sure this is truly a reflection of who you are. However, most companies will have you fill out paperwork before you even get to meet anyone!

Here are a few things you can do that might be consistent with your values:

- Make a big deal of the first day.

- Don't make them fill out paperwork for hours.

- Introduce them around.

- Celebrate based on your values.

- Have other employees explain the values.

- Give them their 30-60-90-180-day expectations or plans.

- Tell them how often you'll follow up.

- Have ALL their equipment ready on the day they start!

We often have goodbye parties or retirement celebrations when people leave. How about having one to reinforce what a good decision they made to join your team? How about one to showcase your values? As they say, you only get one chance to make a first impression. Make it by living your values.

Over at Automation Engineers, Julianna, our once cultural misfit, has become a cultural terrorist. She has completely absconded with the stated cultural values and has reshaped the company to match her values. Ironically, she does not see it this way; she views her role as protecting Roger, and by extension, herself, from all those greedy employees who just "want things."

As with the movie ticket taker she hired as an accounting clerk, most of the employees were in roles way above their skill set or training, with the exception of the engineering department. Julianna hired for expediency, often hiring the first person she interviewed. Her belief was that she would prefer to train people so they would be dependent upon her. If they didn't follow her rules or learn the skill set quickly, she would fire them anyway, although she would keep people who were obedient versus skilled because in her view obedient people were easier to manage. People were disposable, just a means to an end.

The engineering department was the one true area of resistance to Julianna's cultural terrorism. Most of these were senior guys (remember, she called them her "big brains"), and they easily ignored her on most things. She was intimidated by them, and certainly after her disastrous demonstration she did not venture into their world often except to get updates.

Once Julianna had learned of Roger's agreement to sell the company to Jack and Scott after all, she had what was known as the mother of all meltdowns. Roger sat down with Julianna and told her what he had decided. She was heard screaming at him, calling Jack and Scott names, calling Roger stupid, and telling him how they were taking advantage of him, something she actually had a lot of knowledge about! When Roger was impassive, she started crying. Not just crying but wailing. The noise was so upsetting that the entire upstairs office area cleared out. No one wanted to be around when this ended, because they knew it wasn't going to be good.

Roger finally succumbed and had to leave because he couldn't take it anymore. He got his coat and left the building. Julianna followed about fifteen minutes later. As this was mid-morning, no one was quite sure what was going on or what to do, although, with the conversation that had been heard, most could guess that Roger was selling. Since it was common knowledge that Jack and Scott wanted to buy it, everyone was hoping that was going to be the outcome.

The next morning, Julianna and Roger both showed back up at work as if nothing had happened. No one had done any work since the mother of all meltdowns, because they really didn't know if they would have jobs when it was all sorted out. Julianna had a Cheshire-cat grin on her face, so the betting pool was that she was not going anywhere. Roger called Jack and Scott to tell them that unless they hired Julianna and gave her ten percent of the new business he could not sell to them. He would instead sell to Julianna for the same price but let her buy it with the profits of the business over time and on a note.

Jack and Scott were stunned, to say the least. Of all the outcomes they had thought might be possible, this was not one of them. Now they needed to decide what to do since the ultimate cultural misfit and terrorist, Julianna, had completely and wholly taken over the company, literally and culturally.

Chapter Six

Role of the CEO as
Culture Strategist

The role of the CEO or leader in the organization is vital to the survival of the culture. Everyone watches what the leader does and what the leader says. The old saying that actions speak louder than words is especially true when it comes to the role of the leader in a company's culture. Leaders who know this lead with values, which are almost always aligned with those of the organization.

Good leaders know who they are and what their values are, not who people think they should be and what people think their values should be. Only authentic leadership can steer an organization on a course set by the organization's values. Being an executive is all about leadership; it's not about control or power. Although leaders certainly have these at their disposal, the values of the organization will dictate when each can or should be used. Leadership is the ability to inspire others to rally around your culture and mission, and to work toward a shared vision with you. The leader is the culture strategist and becomes the steward of intentional culture.

In this role, the leader's two primary jobs are to grow the company and to grow the people. As the cultural strategist, if this growth is not grounded in the values and culture of the organization, the resulting strategy is not aligned with the culture, and people are cultural misfits. Leaders sometimes think they need to be good at all the top roles in the organization. It's a myth. This leads to micromanagement and an unconscious hiring of people who are not as smart as the leader, and reinforces the leader's omnipotence. Leaders who are culture strategists know what experience or expertise they bring to the table. For example, sales, marketing, finance, operations, strategy, acquisition, and HR are all areas of knowledge that will help, but their most important role is keeping the company aligned with its values through people and growth strategies.

As the Culture Strategist, One Should:

Identify Personal and Company Values

The first step is for the leader to identify his or her own values and check against that of the organization. Are they a fit? If not, it's time to assess whether the leader needs to leave or embrace the company values or, in some cases, engage in a culture change to get more alignment. If it's the founder, one would hope the values are the same. In poor Roger's case, they started off the same, but he ignored his role as culture strategist and let someone change the values. He never stepped back in to take the reins, leading to his own detriment, both personally and financially.

Align Values with Mission and Vision

Ensure that the mission and vision are consistent with the values and are communicated frequently, both internally and externally. If the values don't serve the mission or vision, one or the other needs to change so that all are aligned and create a story that can be told and, hopefully, is inspiring.

Ensure All Policies, Procedures, and Strategies Are Aligned with the Values

This checkpoint would be to see if the values are being owned and respected in all aspects of the organization. How do they show up? How is the leader personally setting the example in the areas that he or she controls? Is the board made up of people who share the values? Is the strategy being set based on the values? Are goals and performance set and monitored based on company values? Are you hiring and firing based on adherence to the values? All are things a leader should be thinking about as the culture strategist or keeper of the culture.

Another area a leader should be looking at is their executive team. These are the people who can implement the culture as an extension of the leader. I usually tell the CEO to take a look at his or her team and ask themselves, knowing what they know now, if they would still hire them today. If the answer is no, they need to be gone, today. Had Roger taken a look at Julianna within this frame, she would never have been allowed to take over and remake the culture of Automation Engineers.

Communicate, Communicate, Communicate!

The culture leader becomes the cheerleader with unwavering belief in the organization and its cultural foundation. There should be no hesitation to use this foundation for growth and to shout it from the rooftops. The brand, the employees, and all the previous steps should be talked about, talked up, and shared constantly. Cultures die when people forget how to tell their stories. Do not let yours die through inattention or hesitation to share your pride in the organization, the people, and its accomplishments.

Walk the Four Corners Constantly

The last thing the culture leader needs to do is constantly check for cultural alignment, adherence to values, and that all is right with the foundation. I can always tell if the company has a winning culture when I am toured around the facility and introduced to the people who make it happen. Get out of your corner office and go talk to the shipping department clerk, the server, the IT guy, the sales person on the road, the introverted coder in the corner. These are your people, those who live the culture, and they are just as important to connect with as are your customers—in fact, more important!

Remember that cultural leaders are leaders, not bosses. Bosses tell people what to do; leaders show people how to do it for themselves. No one likes a boss, but everyone likes good leaders. There is a quote that says, "When a leader is finished, the people think it happened naturally." That's cultural leadership.

BOSSING VS. LEADING

You get the best from people, not by lighting a fire beneath them, but by building a fire within." Bob Nelson

Boss	Leader
Pushes/Drives	Lifts/Supports
Tells/Directs/Lectures	Asks/Requests/Listens
Talks at people	Engages in dialogue with people
Controls through decisions	Facilitates by empowering
Knows the answer	Seeks the answer
Triggers insecurity using fear to achieve compliance	Stimulates creativity using purpose to inspire commitment
Points to errors	Celebrates learning
Problem solver/Decision maker	Collaborator/Facilitator
Delegates responsibility	Models accountability
Creates structure and procedures	Creates vision and flexibility
Does things right	Does right things
Focused on the bottom line	Focused on process that creates the bottom-line results

An Outstanding Cultural Strategist

One organization that has done a great job of cultural strategy with amazing results is Zumiez. Zumiez Inc. is an American specialty clothing store founded by Tom Campion and Gary Haakenson in 1978 and publicly traded since 2005. Both of the original founders largely credit the success of the company to its adherence to their core values. The current CEO has been successful and continues to fulfill that legacy as well.

They define culture as, "A shared set of values evidenced daily over years and decades to define how we want to work with each other, and the kind of environment we want to work in."

Zumiez's Values:

Empowerment

- Each of us is entrusted with, and accountable for, an aspect of the business that is our responsibility.

- Where ownership overlaps, we work toward consensus and collectively refine the ideas we feel are best.

Teaching and Learning

- Our intellectual curiosity compels us to learn how things work and cultivate new skills.

- We recognize this drive in each other, and welcome the responsibility to teach what we've learned and support one another's development.

Recognition

- We like to show appreciation and respect for the hard work of our co-workers.

Fairness and Honesty

- We are free to be truthful with each other.

- We are willing to have the frank conversations that will allow us to resolve our differences and address our opportunities.

Fun

- We enjoy living the values of our culture.

- Facing challenges and finding success together gives us a sense of satisfaction and fulfillment.

- Interestingly, and very cleverly, they have also incorporated values into their brand by identifying "Core Brand Elements."

Zumiez Brand: "The customer's impression of Zumiez is formed collectively by every interaction they have with us across every touchpoint where we engage with them."

Zumiez's Core Brand Elements:

Trend Right

- Applying current trends in a way that suits our customer

- Dedicated to staying on top of trends in fashion, shopping habits, technology, and culture

Unique

- Differentiated from our peers

- Supporting our customers' quest to find and express their unique selves

- Not typical or mainstream

Authentic

- Genuine within the lifestyles we inhabit and true to their subcultures

- Consistently meeting the expectations we raise with our customers

Edgy

- Outside of the comfort zone of the mainstream

- A safe harbor for many varieties of "fringe" kids

- Pushing the limits of mainstream acceptability

Engaging

- Emphasizing human connections and unique experiences as essential touchpoints of the brand

- Opening a dialogue with customers rather than speaking at them

Fun

- Irreverence; not taking ourselves or our message too seriously

- Enjoyment, amusement, lightheartedness

They have taken their Core Values and Brand Elements and created a little booklet that has defined them all. Every new employee gets one. But they've already hired to their values, so everyone is in agreement!

This is a wonderful example of a leader who set and reinforced the organizational values early on so there would be no question as to who they are and how they will act. As a result, the company grew and went public very successfully and is still an industry leader in a very crowded marketspace. The leader was a visionary culture strategist, and it paid off for the entire company.

A contrasting example of a leader as an unintentional culture strategist would be Uber. Travis Kalanick, the founder and CEO, created a host of problems that ranged from a toxic and sexist work culture to pursuing aggressive business practices that often crossed or came very close to the legal line. A technological innovation called Greyball allowed Uber to both track and send a fake app to regulators that might be investigating the company. He was fired by the board in the summer of 2017 when some of the stories came to light—which they always have a way of doing.

So a new CEO, Dara Khosrowshahi, was hired, and to his credit, the first thing he did was set new values:

- We build globally, we live locally. We harness the power and scale of our global operations to deeply connect with the cities, communities, drivers, and riders that we serve, every day.

- We are customer obsessed. We work tirelessly to earn our customers' trust and business by solving their problems, maximizing their earnings, or lowering their costs. We surprise and delight them. We make short-term sacrifices for a lifetime of loyalty.

- We celebrate differences. We stand apart from the average. We ensure people of diverse backgrounds feel welcome. We encourage different opinions and approaches to be heard, and then we come together and build.

- We do the right thing. Period.

- We act like owners. We seek out problems and we solve them. We help each other and those who matter to us. We have a bias for action and accountability. We finish what we start and we build Uber to last. And when we make mistakes, we'll own up to them.

- We persevere. We believe in the power of grit. We don't seek the easy path. We look for the toughest challenges and we push. Our collective resilience is our secret weapon.

- We value ideas over hierarchy. We believe that the best ideas can come from anywhere, both inside and outside our company. Our job is to seek out those ideas, to shape and improve them through candid debate, and to take them from concept to action.

- We make big bold bets. Sometimes we fail, but failure makes us smarter. We get back up, we make the next bet, and we go!

However, much like the previous CEO, they were really nice words but the actions failed to match the words. Shortly after his new values were declared to great public fanfare, it was reported that the new CEO was aware of a data breach that put 57 million Uber customers' personal and financial information at risk for months before he took any initiative to notify affected customers.

As with this case, simply installing a new CEO and creating new values is not going to create a better culture. There are cultural holdouts who will need to be excised before any change really occurs. Both of these CEOs held fast to the culture that had started with the founder: rough, rude, unethical, bullying, win at all costs, and, most importantly, make sure it looks outwardly like something else—until we're caught. You can't put lipstick on that pig fast enough to pretend it's not a pig.

Great leaders understand their role as the culture strategist and leverage it for the growth and good of the organization's people and strategies—ethically. Remember, everyone watches the leader for their cues as to what the organization *really* stands for.

One recent client of mine in Seattle had a small company that was rooted in Hawaiian cultural values. He was reluctant to share these values with his team and was reluctant to really embrace his mission: "Our mission is to develop and maintain positive relationships with our team, clients, and community through quality service, professionalism, and sustainability."

I encouraged him to embrace his values, mission and vision, and stop trying to hide it under a bushel basket. He was afraid the Seattle culture would not be the same. My advice was that it doesn't matter where you are or what you do; your values and organizational culture matter. Customers and employees will be attracted to who you really are, not who you pretend to be. They changed the way they marketed, became a B Corp (social responsibility), and embraced his Hawaiian cultural roots in how he ran his business, and everything changed. The right employees stayed, clients who shared his values showed up, and the business was now on a sustainable growth path versus a slow to no growth plan.

At Automation Engineers, Roger originally had values, but he didn't stand for them. He let himself be steamrolled by Julianna, and therefore, her values, which in some ways were more like the Uber founder's values: get what you want at any cost, no matter the method. Bullying is welcomed and encouraged. Arguably, Roger was the first victim of the new, unintentional culture.

After the dust settled from Julianna's showdown with Roger, Jack and Scott decided that there was no way on earth they were going to allow Julianna to stay if they bought the company. They informed Roger that they could not and would not agree to those terms. Roger was now in a tough spot. He doubted Julianna could really run the company without him, and he also knew that Jack and Scott were going to start a competing company. Neither of these scenarios brought joy to his heart. What was he going to do?

Whenever Roger was at one of these crucial decision points, Julianna knew exactly what to do. She would bully Roger in her own way to get what she wanted, and what she wanted were the reins of the company. Julianna was an extraordinary culture strategist of her own needs and wants. Of course, it worked as it always had, just as she knew it would.

She convinced Roger that she was the right person, that he needed to retire, that this was his only option—she had made sure of that—and that, ultimately, it would be great for him. She alone would safeguard his legacy, as she alone knew how important that was to him. Anyone who is schooled in the basic elements of human psychology knows that as you slowly eliminate all choice from someone, you create learned helplessness. In this final chess move, Julianna had completed her coup of Automation Engineers.

Scott and Jack immediately filed incorporation papers, filed two patents, and got to work trying to put together a team of people to create the company they had always dreamed of. They had signed non-disclosure agreements but had not signed non-compete agreements because Roger didn't believe in enforcing them. And everyone knew that. Julianna's first move as CEO was to send out revised non-compete agreements for everyone to either sign or lose their job. The new intentional culture and values of Automation Engineers were now completely aligned with Julianna, and there was nothing unintentional about it.

Chapter Seven

CULTURE CHANGE

When culture change is discussed in the context of a business, it is often as if it's just one of the many strategic objectives in the annual plan that can be easily checked off the list. It is not. Culture change is hard, if not impossible in some cases.

The reason it's so hard is you have a culture that has veered off course and become something that no one intended (unintentional culture), and most likely performance, productivity, and profits have all fallen off. The slower the downfall of these three measures, the slower people are to react to what is happening, giving more time for the unintentional culture to grow roots. And the deeper the roots, the more resistance to change.

As anyone who has ever dealt with weeds knows, you have to pull them up cleanly by their roots, making sure not to leave any remnants behind, or they'll eventually grow back. Applying this to the business, all those who don't fit the desired new culture must go. But before you do that, you have to identify the culture you would like for the business, the one you and the executive team, board, and shareholders believe would be most successful. As we discussed in Chapter 3, you have to start with the values exercise to identify new values, review what the original values were, keep or enhance them based on what the team believes is aligned with the product or service, and create a communication plan for inside and outside the company.

This is a perfect opportunity to offer severance plans to those who no longer believe in the company's values or aren't willing to change. You will know who they are either by their past poor performance or their resistance to the changes. No one likes change, but cultural misfits or cultural terrorists resist more than anyone else. They became very comfortable in the unintentional culture, and most likely have some degree of power, and now they risk losing it all.

For those who don't leave voluntarily, you'll have to force the issue. It's never pleasant, but like pulling a Band-Aid off, do it quickly and don't be cheap. Regardless of what you feel or think about the person, they are a person, and you will have much less likelihood of a wrongful termination suit if you are generous to them on their way out. You are doing them a favor by making them available to industry with a likelihood that they will find something better suited for their talents and beliefs.

If you don't get rid of all the bad actors who helped create the toxic work environment in the first place, you will end up with a garden full of dandelions that will crowd out all your good plants. It's no different with a cultural misfit. This is truly the hard part, because everyone believes that people can change. Behaviors can change, but if the behavior is rooted in a belief driven by a value, they will likely choose not to. Do you really want to take the risk of hoping that some will embrace the change even though they were part of the problem? Cultural change is an expensive process, and hope is not a strategy.

Another reason people are reluctant to clean house or get rid of as many people as possible is because they say it was a failure of leadership. The real question becomes, once the leader is gone, what values do these employees hold? Those of the unintentional culture that took hold or that of the new culture being created? Only if they share the new values should they be allowed to stay. When Wells Fargo did not get rid of the CEO after the first scandal involving the fake accounts, they signaled it was okay to keep cheating. Eventually, they got rid of him but not the entire board, which should have been held accountable, too. A year later, when the second scandal erupted with unneeded insurance policies being sold to unsuspecting consumers, they still didn't turn over the whole board. They were fined $1 billion for the second scandal. It might have been cheaper to have found some new board members. Sometimes a wholesale house cleaning is in order if you are really going to change a culture. Remember, those roots can go deep when a culture becomes toxic. Weeds are very resistant—just look at all the products we have to eradicate them.

Once you believe you have established shared values and a mission and vision that are aligned, shed the cultural misfits or terrorists, and communicated to everyone inside and outside the company, it's time to set up new processes and procedures to reinforce the values. A complete review of everything that was done in the past is necessary to see what changes, if any, need to be made. No stone can be left unturned, because you don't know where those roots of the old culture may be hiding, just waiting to take hold. Be diligent or weeds will begin to sprout.

One marketing agency here in Seattle was struggling with performance. Once, the company had been known for its edgy, creative genius and innovative ideas, but recently everything seemed flat and "already done." They were once brilliant at creating winning strategies and finding just the right people for each of the many creative roles needed to put a project together, but they had truly lost their edge.

The founder had left the day-to-day management of the agency to someone who had "bought in" to the business a few years back when she needed some cash. The founder figured he was as good as anyone to install as president and he wanted the job and insisted he needed more control to be successful. Although she was not what one would call a good manager or leader by any stretch, she did understand the product, the creative process, the people, and the customers. The new president was a finance expert and knew the numbers inside and out. What he didn't understand, let alone respect, was the creative process. The shock to the culture was profound under his leadership. He instituted new forms and processes for everything and everyone. He mandated that everyone fill out daily activity charts detailing what they had done each day. He also treated them all as interchangeable, not understanding that a brand expert was not a web designer or a graphic design expert. He was an introvert by nature, so all his directives were done via email or by his assistant. This was completely counterintuitive to the creative types who made up the majority of the workforce. They needed to talk things out, to dialogue, to whiteboard, to imagine. He completely missed that the product of this firm was in fact its talented workforce. When he took over, it was about a 200-person firm, and after six months of his leadership, the high-potential creative talent started heading for the exits in droves.

After about a year of this, performance hit a record low, and revenue was declining every month. The VP was vocal about what was happening and decided to take matters into her own hands when she could not get the president to even talk with her about it. She held a values session over three separate days, creating seven values they all agreed on. As it was a creative agency, they made stand-ups for everyone's desks listing the seven values and the meaning. The team was excited about it, but once the president saw what the values actually were, he put a stop to it. The VP pled her case, explaining that to get things back on track they had to get back to who they were. The president still refused to let her implement the new values.

There was a mutiny of the staff, and the VP finally went to

the founder and explained what was going on. She was completely unaware, other than noticing that her dividend payments were much lower than she expected. She came back, fired the president, and installed the VP as president to lead the company. They sold three years later for twice the amount they had been expecting. Values won the day and the share price!

When two organizations merge, there is almost always a dominant culture. That culture will win, regardless of whether it produces. Even if both come in with the same amount of cash, unless their values, mission, and vision are identical, there will be friction and one culture will lose out. This is why bigger companies spend all kinds of money on consultants to help with "cultural integration" when a merger happens. They also pay off their highest performers to stay with them through the change curve, as they don't want to lose them in the middle of the scrum. Often, when smaller companies are acquired, the founder/owners want to make sure the culture is preserved, as they rightly believe it was the key to their success. However, the acquirer might also have a winning culture (obviously they are making acquisitions), so they are not likely to switch to the culture of the company they acquired. Most often, though, when assessing the likelihood of success or failure of an acquisition, the company culture will be looked at closely to see how it is contributing to performance, or whether it is not. And they will look at how similar that culture is to their own. This is the most predictive key indicator of a successful acquisition, because there is less disruption and change for the employees. Smart managers let people leave with nice packages if they don't want to be a part of the new company when an acquisition happens. Better to let them go before you start the integration process.

Organizations change their values over time as well, when they move through the different stages of a business. There are five stages of business growth according to Neil Churchill and Virginal Lewis (HBR #83301):

1. **Existence**: the owner is the business, and it's all about start-up and getting customers.

2. **Survival:** the business hits the breakeven stage but could go either way, grow or go broke.

3. **Success:** the company is making profits and generating cash, and the question becomes: Should they use it as a platform for growth? (Which requires the owners to risk it all again).

4. **Takeoff:** searching how to finance growth; it can be sold or become a big business.

5. **Resource Maturity:** the founder and the business are quite separate, and the business really has become something unattached to him or her personally.

In the first three stages, the values are likely to be the same: getting customers, staying alive, and sharing a vision of what that might look like. The values may change in stages 4 and 5 as acquisitions happen and strategy changes. When the founder is no longer around, the main guardian of the values and culture also leaves. The strength of the intentional culture he or she left behind coupled with the new strategy will determine if those values need to change.

Boeing is one of these businesses that went through all the stages after starting in Seattle in the early 1900s. William Boeing was a pioneer and believed the following:

My firm conviction from the start has been that science and hard work can lick what appear to be insurmountable difficulties. I've tried to make the men around me feel, as I do, that we are embarked as pioneers upon a new science and industry in which our problems are so new and unusual that it behooves no one to dismiss any novel idea with the statement that it can't be done. —William Boeing

He also had a plaque outside his wall that was a quote from Hippocrates:

1. There is no authority except facts.

2. Facts are obtained by accurate observation.

3. Deductions are to be made only from facts.

4. Experience has proved the truth of these rules.

Boeing (the man and the company) exhibited these values and beliefs in the early days and grew the company until he got it to Stage 5, at which point he retired and left the business to the businessmen, not pilots and aviation enthusiasts like him. The values of the larger publicly traded organization are different. There are shareholders, multiple departments, and many leaders, so the scrappy values and behaviors that got it to that point were not likely to get it to the next phase. Understanding that cultures and values will change as the business goes through growth cycles will reinforce the need to revisit them at each phase.

One of the lessons from Boeing is that, as the founder, he knew when to take his exit. He knew when it was time to leave to live his values and let the company live out its new stages: take off and resource maturity. A frequent issue for companies moving through the stages—or, more accurately, getting stuck—is founder loyalty. A founder will often be very loyal to those employees whom he or she believes helped get the business going, even when the organization has long surpassed the individual skill sets. Such was the case with Roger at Automation Engineers and Julianna. Roger could not ignore what he perceived to be her contribution to the organization and did not see that she was not qualified for the role and responsibilities she had been given. This loyalty was ultimately what caused Roger to never grow the company and achieve his original vision. The company got stuck in success and never moved on.

Generational family businesses are no exception. Most people will agree that by the time a business gets to the third generation, things have changed, and often not for the better. The grandchildren will not automatically share the values of the founders and will likely have different ideas. When they take the reins, they will be running it based on their values, not always those of the founders. This is neither good nor bad, but it needs to be identified and called out. Third-generation companies can have entitled leaders who have no idea what the original founders went through to get it started. I wonder what Sam Walton would think of Walmart today, a company that sources more than seventy-five percent of their products from overseas, when one of his founding principles was "Buy American for Americans"—not to mention the number of small businesses it has put out of business.

One of the most profound examples of the power of values for me was when I was a member of a CEO group, called TEC at the time and now Vistage, that was owned and led by a scrappy group of former CEOs. TEC started a CEO peer group organization, where the membership model contracted with former CEOs to facilitate CEO groups that each of them was responsible for building. This brought CEOs of small to mid-sized businesses together each month for an all-day meeting to hear speakers, learn from one another, and help each other solve issues and take advantage of opportunities. They also were given coaching from the Chair, or facilitator, of the group each month. They paid monthly dues that were split about one third to the speakers, one third to the organization, and one third to the Chair. After about forty years, they had created a very profitable business in all fifty states and several other countries. The founders were all ready to retire and decided to sell the business. They ended up selling to Michael Milken, the junk bond king who, although brilliant, was convicted for SEC violations. He was out of jail and rebuilding his image through education acquisitions and thought TEC was the perfect executive leadership education organization to round out his portfolio.

TEC/Vistage started with the values of trust, caring, challenge, and growth, and was very much about the leader, or Chair, of the groups and its members. The groups were private; nothing was shared outside of the groups. In fact, most didn't know who the members were or where they were other than their own group. Milken saw it as an opportunity to market to the 10,000 members. Not only did all the members revolt but the Chairs threatened to quit as well, so the decision was quickly reversed and the CEO that Milken had installed was moved out in favor of a former Chair, whom the community loved and trusted. Fortunately, it was a very profitable company, so it weathered the transition—and a pretty big black eye. Trust had been violated but ultimately restored, so everyone was back on track.

Fast-forward a few years and Milken wanted to sell, but the growth rate was not fast enough for him or investors. The ten-percent year-after-year growth was deemed to be too slow. He replaced the CEO once again, installing a former TV executive who did not have experience with small to mid-size businesses (the customers). He proceeded to round out his executive team with other like-minded individuals, all seasoned executives but none of whom had ever started or run an entrepreneurial business. They treated the values like nice-to-haves but did not truly understand or believe they were what made the business work. To the new CEO's credit, he did try to understand the entrepreneurs and the Chairs (who were contractors, not employees), but a similar effort was not made by the rest of the leadership team.

I was brought on in 2008 as an SVP, after having been a successful Chair, to help with the "cultural divide," as they called it. There was a disconnect between those who delivered the product, the members who were the customers, and HQ. The answer was to have more executives with experience in the field. What I found was that, although we were a leadership development organization, leadership was the one thing we didn't do well. There was a belief that the field and therefore the members were somehow less than or not as good as the executive team. The field understood this belief, but for the most part, it didn't affect them as independent contractors. They just kept doing what they always did and let HQ spin. And spin it did.

The disconnect between the stated values lived in the field versus those lived at HQ was stark. HQ was a revolving door of talent. Anyone who came from the field was discounted as being "one of them," so somehow not equivalent to the leadership. The organization remained very profitable, which covered up lots of mistakes and failed projects. The irony was of course that if the leadership team had only fully embraced the values that were lived by the one thousand plus Chairs in the field, growth would have been exponential, and Milken would have achieved the multiple he so badly wanted. Eventually it did sell, but not for what they wanted, and the leadership team was changed out for a new set of investors.

This was a case of the leadership badly wanting to change the culture to one of fast growth but failing to realize that the reason it had existed and grown in the first place was its values, which were deeply held and owned by the field, the heart of the business. Had the leadership realized and embraced this understanding, they would have become the most amazing support organization to the field and resource organization to the members. Growth would have been the result. Remember, the values were trust, caring, challenge, and growth, and they still are. The field made sure of it. The Chairs, members, and most employees were drawn to the organization based on its values, and they were not going away, regardless of leadership changes.

Over at Automation Engineers, with the takeover of the culture complete, most of the remaining employees were no longer hoping for a cultural change. It was now clear that Julianna was in charge, and hope that Jack and Scott would rescue them was fading. And now even Roger was gone, so there was no one to act as a compass, albeit a faulty one.

The CFO continued to tell Julianna that her "helping" herself to dividends on top of the recent sales tax audit that left them with a huge tax bill and fine left no additional cash for a buyout from Roger. As Julianna did not really understand the financial statements, she just told him to figure it out. By the end of the first week with Julianna officially at the helm, the company had no more cash reserves and sales were down ten percent from the previous year. The CFO saw no way out except borrowing and didn't think Julianna had the assets to secure a bank loan. He gave his notice.

Meanwhile, Jack and Scott were happily moving on with their own new company. In fact, they were thrilled that, although things were very tight, they no longer had the specter of continued chaos over their heads with Julianna's constant micromanaging. They had managed to hire ten former AE employees and had secured enough funding for one year. With the employees on board and the values, mission, and vision set, they were ready to go for some new clients.

That was until they received a cease-and-desist order from Julianna, who was suing them for breach of contract, patent infringement, and violation of their NDAs. Although Roger never believed in suing people, because it was too expensive and unlikely to be fruitful, Julianna had no such doubts.

Chapter Eight

THE LEGACY OF A CULTURE

Entrepreneurs rarely start a business with a cultural legacy in mind. Often, it's about survival, an innovation, the thrill of the ride, making money, or not wanting to have a boss other than themselves. *But what happens when we start with the end in mind?* What can be created through a solid vision and culture that results in something that lives well beyond the original founder or idea? That's cultural legacy, the lasting reputation of the organization.

Think of those iconic brands or companies that changed the world: IBM, Apple, HP, Boeing, Amazon, Pan American, Facebook, RCA, GE, and the list goes on. The products or innovations these companies created would never have survived had there not been a strong, functional culture at the organization's foundation. At the root of the culture were solid values, ones that survived the founders. It's not just what people say about you; it's the legacy of the company itself. How has it changed the lives of the people who have used the products or services? How has it changed the lives of the employees? The shareholders? The vendors?

In Seattle, we are overrun with what are dubbed "Microsofties" and "Microsoft millionaires," and now "Amazonians." In the early days of Microsoft stock was given out generously, so purchasing agents became millionaires and retired at thirty-five. I remember being in my thirties and working with one of these people, thinking, How did this happen? They admitted the work was sometimes brutal, but the payoff was amazing. Years later I was at a fundraiser and ran into one of these early Microsoft retirees. He had become a philanthropist and traveled extensively. There are thousands of these early retirees who have created unrealistic beliefs about this being the norm. Microsoft inadvertently created a legacy for themselves by having many, many early retirees who just happened to be in the right place at the time. Their children have come to see this as "the way it is."

These behemoth tech companies are rare, and most small businesses are not going to create legacies similar to these. However, you can create something that you will be proud of and whose cultural legacy lives on beyond you, the founder. When I work with entrepreneurs, especially young executives, I tell them the one thing they have that no one can ever take from them is their reputation. It is theirs to guard, theirs to keep, and theirs to give away, as they often unintentionally do. The same can be said for a business. Every action, reaction, and interaction says something about your company, and it can't be undone, only explained. What is the story that will be told about your company? What will your legacy be?

The cultural legacy of many of the companies I work with ends up being about the CEO or founder and not about the company. Think about Roger at Automation Engineers. By abdicating his values, his reputation became about what he had let happen to an otherwise good company, not about the products themselves.

I was brought in by the board to work with a new CEO in a family business. The company was over a hundred years old and had created an innovative sealant that had multiple patents and had stood the test of time. The company had close to $100M in sales worldwide, but the board was concerned that the new CEO was not up to the task. He was the third generation; his grandfather was the founder. He had no education other than on the job. What struck me about the business was that it was like stepping into a time capsule. Everything was exactly how his grandfather had left it. It reminded me more of a museum than of a business. The majority of the employees had been with them for at least twenty-five years or more, and their parents before them had worked there as well.

What I found was that, although the new CEO was willing to make changes and get back to their innovative foundation, both of his parents (in their eighties and still working in the business) did not believe that anything should change. Remarkably, the mother was still doing the accounting with handwritten ledgers. She would give everything to the outside accounting firm once a month, and they would balance the books and produce the statements. They did have an automated production system, but the software was twenty years old and on a mainframe, and there were literally no vendors left who knew how to service it. The company was fading because no one knew how to move on from the founder's vision. He had never empowered anyone to make decisions, so everyone had just kept doing things the same way for a hundred years! They did what they had been told to do. The only reason there was a board was that the founder had wisely enshrined it in the incorporation papers so the bank was obligated to continue it.

The most difficult challenge I had was to help the new CEO (who was in his mid-fifties) understand that he in fact did have the ability to make changes, that his ideas were good, and that if he did not speak up his grandfather's business would be gone—the legacy, gone. We went back to his grandfather's original values—innovation, service to others, respect, and ingenuity—and I asked him where it said that no one could change things. He needed to innovate or watch the company die. For all their employees and customers whom they were in service to, he needed to make decisions, and out of respect to his grandfather, he had to bring the business up to date. He "retired" his parents, made massive changes to the processes and systems, brought in outsiders, and started looking at acquisitions. He was on fire and honoring the legacy of his grandfather in the process. Fortunately, the company was awash in cash. A side benefit of "no change" was that since no money had been spent on updating systems over the years, they had plenty to spare!

This business had a good-news ending, but in most cases the opposite happens. My business was one of them. I became an owner of the business by executing a turnaround. I was running one of the branch offices of a business that was losing money due mostly to inattention by the owner/founder and an over-diversification of product lines. The owner came down to the branch and wanted to meet with me, which I assumed meant our branch was to be closed or I was going to be fired. Surprisingly, she wanted to leverage my mergers and acquisitions background to help her sell the business or at least sell the inventory. With what I knew about the business, I let her know there was not much to sell, and due to the aging of the inventory, maybe ten cents on the dollar was all she could expect if we liquidated. I gave her a third alternative: I asked her to let me try to turn it around, and if I did, I wanted a stake in the business. Six months later, I had turned the business around to break even, and before the year was out we were generating a profit again. I went back to the core values of the business: collaboration, expertise, innovation, and trust, and I reintroduced these to the team and shed all the product lines that did not fit. We only had to let five people go, and the team produced miracles together. It was one of my proudest moments, for the team and the company.

I had sorted us out for the moment and had acquired a forty-percent stake in the business, but as a distributor in a crowded field, it was only a matter of time before we hit another crisis. We needed to acquire or be acquired. Because our cash reserves were limited, acquiring another business was out of the question.

However, we were a good acquisition target. I found a big player who would benefit from our expertise and market presence, and they were interested. We went through all the due diligence and got down to the final deal points. At our final meeting my partner, who had been supportive and approving up until this point, asked about their strategy. They patiently explained again what the rollup would look like, our roles, and the larger nationwide strategy. She stood up, slowly pushed her chair back, and said, "That's the stupidest strategy I've ever heard," and walked out of the room. Needless, to say, it was an awkward moment. I was so stunned, I didn't know what to do, but the CEO of the other company smiled and said, "Well, I guess we're done here," shook hands, and walked out.

I went back to my office, shell shocked. My partner waltzed in, all smiles, and said, "We don't need them. Did you hear what they said? We can do that ourselves without them!" This was possibly even more stunningly stupid than what she had just done in the meeting. I just looked at her and shook my head. I made it clear I was not going to be on board for that journey. A month later, I was gone. This was a "hell no" moment for me. I then found out exactly how much value forty-percent minority ownership of a privately held company was worth. Almost nothing. Had the deal gone through, it would have been worth close to $2M in shares, cash, and a job. The large company called one last time to see if my partner had changed her mind, and when I informed him that she had not, he laughed and said, "Well, I gave you full warning what we're going to do." He went on to do exactly that and decimated my old company.

The valuable lesson I learned from that experience early on in my career was that entrepreneurs sometimes have an end in mind, but it's unstated. More often, they don't have an end in mind, so when opportunity knocks they don't know what to do. I also learned that they often have stated business values that are nothing more than posters on the wall and meaningless for all practical purposes.

My partner was not interested in a legacy for the company; she only wanted to keep the business forever and let it die when she was done working. I was just a means to that end, nothing more and nothing less. I belatedly realized that she had told me what she needed to in order to get my help, and unfortunately I was naive enough to believe it. Almost immediately, the business shrank to less than half of what it had been, and she blamed me for it, but everyone who had been there knew what really happened. I still have a plaque on my wall with etched signatures from all the employees for my leadership in turning the ship around. I will not fault her for what she wanted, and I have long since forgiven her for her misrepresentations. I learned valuable lessons on multiple fronts and have used those many times in work with other companies. In this case, the lack of a stated legacy should have been a clue to me.

Interestingly, I also learned that I was not the first person she had used in this manner. There was a former partner before me who had an eerily similar path. The personal legacy she left was one of dishonesty. (At one point, I had to fire her boyfriend and an employee she was having an affair with.) I was not without my share of mistakes in the process, but I kept my reputation and refused to violate my values: caring, creativity, curiosity, authenticity, and doing the right thing at all times. *Authenticity* means owning your mistakes, being true to who you are, and, for me, forgiving myself and others for an imperfect journey.

Everyone, no matter where they are in an organization, leaves a personal legacy. When you hear the "remember so and so," or the old stories that always involve a person, those are personal legacy stories. Eventually, all those stories merge to create the legacy of a company. Remember the Uber CEO? His "bro culture" almost brought down the whole company, and instead of being known for innovation and changing how we all get rides, we think about his bad behavior. Companies with good, strong, intentional, and defined cultures leave aligned legacies for the organization. Companies with toxic, dysfunctional, unintentional cultures leave legacies that are about bad behaviors gone wild.

Define Your Legacy

As we started this chapter with "begin with the end in mind" and this book with "how to create a culture that works" (meaning connected to results), think about the legacy that you want to create in your business. How do you want your company to be remembered? *Who* do you want to be remembered as? What is the cultural legacy you want to leave as an imprint on your family, your employees, your customers, and your town? If you are an entrepreneur, you own the legacy. It's your personal and business reputation to build or to give away.

Roger at Automation Engineers gave his cultural legacy away along with his reputation. He refused to stand up to the cultural misfit, who soon became a cultural terrorist, who held him hostage and kept him from his dreams. His frustration grew, and his inability to confront or eliminate the cultural cancer of Julianna from his business created a whole new reputation for himself and his company, one that he never intended.

Scott and Jack hired a lawyer to combat Julianna's lawsuit and sought to reassure their investors that they could win on all accounts. The lawyers seemed to think they had a solid case. To their surprise, the attorneys wanted to reach out to Roger directly, since he was not listed as a party in the lawsuit, and see what he would say. Interestingly, he was willing to talk, and not only that, he was willing to side with them. Scott and Jack were shocked that Roger was willing to go against Julianna and wondered why at this end stage of the game he would finally get some resolve to do the right thing.

What they found out was that, in the three months since they had been gone, Julianna had run out of cash, could not get financing without a signature from Roger (which he refused to give), multiple employees had walked out, and after the CFO left, the result was chaos in the finance department. In a nutshell, Julianna was close to having to shut the doors, so the lawsuit was going nowhere, and Roger was not going to bail her out. All Roger wanted was for Jack and Scott to buy up the assets—the old patents—take on as many Automation Engineers employees as possible, and build their company into the automation expert that Roger had always hoped would be his legacy. All he asked was that they keep the names of some of his favorite products—not a heavy lift for Scott and Jack.

True to his word, he did not bail Julianna out, and when she defaulted on the ridiculously impossible note she owed Roger, he took back control of the business and shut the doors. Rather than sell all the assets to Jack and Scott, he decided to just give them the rights to all his patents. In the end, he would be known for his final act of decency, and Jack and Scott went on to create the best automation products in the industry, aligned with their values and grounded in the hard-won knowledge that culture matters, values matter, and if you build and run your business based on those you will always have a solid foundation.

Acknowledgements

Writing and speaking about business culture over the last 10 years is the result of all the amazing entrepreneurs I have met and learned from along the way. I would like to thank each of these entrepreneurs for allowing me to be curious and ask about their success, and their generous sharing of those stories.

I would specifically like to thank Tod Johnson, CEO of Lee Johnson Auto Family in Washington State for his contribution to Automation Engineers. He also spent many hours helping to edit and read the book for me from a CEO perspective. Their business is built on family values and thrives because of his great stewardship of those values.

I'd also like to thank Kim Obbink, my writing partner of the "How NOT to be a Leader" series, for encouraging me to write and speak about Culture. She has always inspired teams by leading with values and has been an inspiration to me!

Lastly, thank you to all my family and friends who put up with me being too busy "writing" to do other things and encouraging me to keep going, no matter what!